A Bold Stroke for a Husband by Hannah Cowley

A Comedy in Five Acts

As Performed at the THEATRE ROYAL, COVENT GARDEN, & THE PARK THEATRE, NEW YORK.

Hannah Cowley was born Hannah Parkhouse on March 14th, 1743, the daughter of Hannah (née Richards) and Philip Parkhouse, a bookseller in Tiverton, Devon.

As one might expect details of much of her life are scant and that of her early life almost non-existent.

However, we do know that she married Thomas Cowley and that the couple moved to London where Thomas worked as an official in the Stamp Office and as a part-time journalist.

Her career in the literary world seemed to happen rather late. It was whilst the couple were attending a play, thought to be sometime in late 1775, that Cowley was struck by a sudden necessity to write.

Her first play, a comedy called The Runaway was sent to the famed actor-manager, David Garrick. It was produced at his final season at the Drury Lane theatre on February 15th, 1776. It was a success. She wrote her next two plays, the farce, Who's the Dupe? and the tragedy, Albina, before the year was out.

Getting these two plays into production took much longer and involved a very public spat with her rival Hannah More over whether Cowley's works had been plagarised by More.

Cowley wrote her most popular comedy in 1780; The Belle's Stratagem. It was staged at Covent Garden.

Her next play, The World as It Goes; or, a Party at Montpelier (the title was later changed to Second Thoughts Are Best) was unsuccessful, but she continued to write and there followed another seven plays; Which is the Man?; A Bold Stroke for a Husband; More Ways Than One; A School for Greybeards, or, The Mourning Bride; The Fate of Sparta, or, The Rival Kings; A Day in Turkey, or, The Russian Slaves and The Town Before You.

In 1801 Cowley published perhaps her greatest poetical work. A six-book epic "The Siege of Acre: An Epic Poem".

That same year Cowley retired to Tiverton in Devon, where she spent her remaining years out of the public spotlight whilst she quietly revised her plays.

Hannah Cowley died of liver failure on March 11th, 1809.

Index of Contents

DRAMATIS PERSONÆ

	Covent Garden.	Park, New York, 1830.
Don Cæsar	Mr. Munden	Mr. Barnes.
Don Julio	Mr. Lewis	Mr. Simpson.
Don Carlos	Mr. Cooke	Mr. Barry.
Don Vincentio	Mr. Fawcet	Mr. Richings.
Don Garcia	Mr. Brunton	Mr. Woodhull.
Don Vasquez	Mr. Simmons	Mr. Foot.
Gasper	Mr. Blanchard	Mr. Blakeley.
Pedro	Mr. Harley	Mr. Nexsen.
Servants	{Mr. Hayden.	{Mr. Bissett.
Donna Olivia	Mrs. Glover	Miss Fisher.
Donna Victoria	Mrs. Litchfield	Mrs. Hilson.
Donna Laura	Mrs. Dibdin	Mrs. Durie.
Minette	Mrs. Gibbs	Mrs. Wheatley.
Marcella	Miss Waddy	Mrs. Godey.
Sancha	Mrs. Whitmore	Miss Turnbull.
Inis	Mrs. Beverly	Miss Jessup.

SCENE—Spain

STAGE DIRECTIONS

EXITS AND ENTRANCES
R. means Right; L. Left; F. the Flat, or Scene running across the back of the Stage; D. F. Door in Flat; R. D. Right Door; L. D. Left Door; S. E. Second Entrance; U. E. Upper Entrance; C. D. Centre Door.

RELATIVE POSITIONS
R. means Right; L. Left; C. Centre; R. C. Right of Centre; L. C. Left of Centre.

The Reader is supposed to be on the Stage, facing the Audience.

REMARKS by Mrs Elizabeth Inchbald

Although "The Bold Stroke for a Husband," by Mrs. Cowley, does not equal "The Bold Stroke for a Wife," by Mrs. Centlivre, either in originality of design, wit, or humour, it has other advantages more honourable to her sex, and more conducive to the reputation of the stage.

Here is contained no oblique insinuation, detrimental to the cause of morality—but entertainment and instruction unite, to make a pleasant exhibition at a theatre, or give an hour's amusement in the closet.

Plays, where the scene is placed in a foreign country, particularly when that country is Spain, have a license to present certain improbabilities to the audience, without incurring the danger of having them called such; and the authoress, by the skill with which she has used this dramatic permittance, in making the wife of Don Carlos pass for a man, has formed a most interesting plot, and embellished it with lively, humorous, and affecting incident.

Still there is another plot, of which Olivia is the heroine, as Victoria is of the foregoing; and this more comic fable, in which the former is chiefly concerned, seems to have been the favourite story of the authoress, as from this she has taken her title.

But if Olivia makes a bold stroke to obtain a husband, surely Victoria makes a still bolder, to preserve one; and there is something less honourable in the enterprises of the young maiden, in order to renounce her state, than in those of a married woman to avert the dangers that are impending over hers.

Whichever of those females becomes the most admired object with the reader, he will not be insensible to the trials of the other, or to the various interests of the whole dramatis personæ, to whom the writer has artfully given a kind of united influence; and upon a happy combination it is, that sometimes, the success of a drama more depends, than upon the most powerful support of any particularly prominent, yet insulated, character.

The part of Don Vincentio was certainly meant as a moral satire upon the extravagant love or the foolish affectation, of pretending to love, to extravagance—music. This satire was aimed at so many, that the shaft struck none. The charm of music still prevails in England, and the folly of affected admirers.

Vincentio talks music, and Don Julio speaks poetry. Such, at least, is his fond description of his mistress Olivia, in that excellent scene in the third act, where she first takes off her veil, and fascinates him at once by the force of her beauty.

In the delineation of this lady, it is implied that she is no termagant, although she so frequently counterfeits the character. This insinuation the reader, if he pleases, may trust—but the man who would venture to marry a good impostor of this kind, could not excite much pity, if his helpmate was often induced to act the part which she had heretofore, with so much spirit, assumed.

The impropriety of making fraud and imposition necessary evils, to counteract tyranny and injustice, is the fault of all Spanish dramas—and perhaps the only one which attaches to the present comedy.

A BOLD STROKE FOR A HUSBAND

ACT I

SCENE I.—A Street in Madrid

Enter **SANCHA** from a House, R. D. She advances, then runs back, and beckons to **PEDRO** within.

SANCHA
Hist! Pedro! Pedro!

[Enter **PEDRO**, R. D.

There he is: dost see him? just turning by St. Antony in the corner. Now, do you tell him that your mistress is not at home; and if his jealous donship should insist on searching the house, as he did yesterday, say that somebody is ill—the black has got a fever, or that—

PEDRO
Pho, pho, get you in. Don't I know that the duty of a lacquey in Madrid is to lie with a good grace? I have been studying it now for a whole week, and I'll defy don or devil to surprise me into a truth. Get you in, I say—here he comes.

[Exit **SANCHA**, R. D. F.

[Enter **CARLOS**, L.

[**PEDRO** struts up to him.]

Donna Laura is not at home, sir.

CARLOS
Not at home!—come, sir, what have you received for telling that lie?

PEDRO
Lie!—lie!—Signior!—

CARLOS
It must be a lie, by your promptness in delivering it.—What a fool does your mistress trust—A clever rascal would have waited my approach, and, delivering the message with easy coolness, deceived me—thou hast been on the watch, and runnest towards me with a face of stupid importance, bawling, that she may hear through the lattice how well thou obeyest her,—"Donna Laura is not at home, sir."

PEDRO
Hear through the lattice—hah! by'r lady, she must have long ears, to reach from the grotto in the garden to the street.

CARLOS
Hah! [Seizes him.] Now, sir, your ears shall be longer, if you do not tell me who is with her in the grotto.

PEDRO
In the grotto, sir!—did I say any thing about the grotto? I—I only meant that—

CARLOS
Fool!—dost thou trifle with me? who is with her?

[Pinching his ear.]

PEDRO
Oh!—why, nobody, sir—only the pretty young gentleman's valet, waiting for an answer to a letter he brought. There! I have saved my ears at the expense of my place. I have worn this fine coat but a week, and I shall be sent back to Segovia for not being able to lie, though I have been learning the art six days and nights.

CARLOS
Well—come this way—if thou wilt promise to be faithful to me, I will not betray thee: nor at present enter the house.

PEDRO
Oh, sir, blessings on you!

CARLOS
How often does the pretty young gentleman visit her?

PEDRO
Every day, sir—If he misses, madam's stark wild.

CARLOS
Where does he live?

PEDRO
Truly, I know not, sir.

CARLOS
How! [Menacing.]

PEDRO
By the honesty of my mother, I cannot tell, sir. She calls him Florio;—that's his christian name—his heathen name I never heard.

CARLOS
You must acquaint me when they are next together.

PEDRO
Lord, sir, if there should be any blood spilt!

CARLOS
Promise,—or I'll lead thee by the ears to the grotto.

PEDRO
I promise, I promise.

CARLOS
There, take that, [Gives money.] and if thou art faithful, I'll treble it. Now go in and be a good lad—and, d'ye hear?—you may tell lies to every body else, but remember you must always speak truth to me.

PEDRO
I will, sir,—I will. [Exit, looking at the money, R. D. F.

CARLOS
'Tis well my passion is extinguished, for I can now act with coolness; I'll wait patiently, for the hour of their security, and take them in the softest moments of their love. But if ever I trust to woman more—may every—

[Enter two **WOMEN**, veiled, followed by **JULIO**, R.

JULIO
Fie, ladies! keep your curtains drawn so late! The sun is up—'tis time to look abroad—[Tries to remove the veils.] Nay, if you are determined on night and silence, I take my leave. A woman without prattle, is like burgundy without spirit.—Bright eyes, to touch me, must belong to sweet tongues.

[Going, R. **LADIES** exit L.

CARLOS

Sure, 'tis Julio. Hey!

JULIO [Returning.]
Don Carlos? Yes, by all the sober gods of matrimony!—Why, what business, goodman gravity, canst thou have in Madrid? I understand you are married—quietly settled in your own pastures—father of a family, and the instructive companion of country vine dressers—ha! ha!

CARLOS
'Tis false, by Heaven!—I have forsworn the country—left my family, and run away from my wife.

JULIO
Really! then matrimony has not totally destroyed thy free will.

CARLOS
'Tis with difficulty I have preserved it though; for women, thou knowest, are most unreasonable beings! as soon as I had exhausted my stock of love tales, which, with management, lasted beyond the honey-moon, madam grew sullen,—I found home dull, and amused myself with the pretty peasants of the neighbourhood—Worse and worse!—we had nothing now but faintings, tears and hysterics, for twenty-four honey-moons more.—So one morning I gave her in her sleep a farewell kiss, to comfort her when she should awake, and posted to Madrid; where, if it was not for the remembrance of the clog at my heel, I should bound o'er the regions of pleasure, with more spirit than a young Arabian on his mountains.

JULIO
Do you find this clog no hindrance in affairs of gallantry?

CARLOS
Not much.—In that house there—but, damn her, she's perfidious!—in that house is a woman of beauty, with pretensions to character and fortune, who devoted herself to my passion.

JULIO
If she's perfidious, give her to the winds.

CARLOS
Ah, but there is a rub, Julio, I have been a fool—a woman's fool!—In a state of intoxication, she wheedled me, or rather cheated me, out of a settlement.

JULIO
Pho! is that—

CARLOS
Oh! but you know not its nature. A settlement of lands, that both honour and gratitude ought to have preserved sacred from such base alienation. In short, if I cannot recover them, I am a ruined man.

JULIO
Nay, this seems a worse clog than t'other—Poor Carlos! So bewived and be—

CARLOS

Pr'ythee, have compassion.

[Enter a **SERVANT**, R. with a letter to **JULIO**; he reads it, and then nods to the **SERVANT**, who exits, R.

CARLOS
An appointment, I'll be sworn, by that air of mystery and satisfaction—come, be friendly, and communicate.

JULIO [Putting up the letter.]
You are married, Carlos;—that's all I have to say—you are married.

CARLOS
Pho! that's past long ago, and ought to be forgotten; but if a man does a foolish thing once, he'll hear of it all his life.

JULIO
Ay, the time has been when thou might'st have been intrusted with such a dear secret,—when I might have opened the billet, and feasted thee with the sweet meandering strokes at the bottom, which form her name, when—

CARLOS
What, 'tis from a woman then?

JULIO
It is.

CARLOS
Handsome?

JULIO
Hum—not absolutely handsome, but she'll pass, with one who has not had his taste spoiled by—matrimony.

CARLOS
Malicious dog!—Is she young?

JULIO
Under twenty—fair complexion, azure eyes, red lips, teeth of pearl, polished neck, fine turned shape, graceful—

CARLOS
Hold, Julio, if thou lov'st me!—Is it possible she can be so bewitching a creature?

JULIO
'Tis possible—though, to deal plainly, I never saw her: but I love my own pleasure so well, that I could fancy all that, and ten times more.

CARLOS

What star does she inhabit?

JULIO

'Faith, I know not; my orders are to be in waiting, at seven, at the Prado.

CARLOS

Prado!—hey!—gad! can't you take me with you? for though I have forsworn the sex myself, and have done with them for ever, yet I may be of use to you, you know.

JULIO

'Faith, I can't see that—however, as you are a poor wo-begone married mortal, I'll have compassion, and suffer thee to come.

CARLOS

Then I am a man again! Wife, avaunt! mistress, farewell!—At seven, you say!

JULIO

Exactly.

CARLOS

I'll meet thee at Philippi!

[Exeunt, **JULIO**, L. **CARLOS**, R.

SCENE II.—A Spacious Garden, Belonging to Don Caesar

Enter **MINETTE** and **INIS**, R. 2d E.

MINETTE

There, will that do! My lady sent me to make her up a nosegay; these orange flowers are delicious, and this rose, how sweet?

INIS

Pho! what signifies wearing sweets in her bosom, unless they would sweeten her manners?—'tis amazing you can be so much at your ease; one might think your lady's tongue was a lute, and her morning scold an agreeable serenade.

MINETTE

So they are—Custom, you know. I have been used to her music now these two years, and I don't believe I could relish my breakfast without it.

INIS

I would rather never break my fast, than do it on such terms. What a difference between your mistress and mine! Donna Victoria is as much too gentle, as her cousin is too harsh.

MINETTE

Ay, and you see what she gets by it; had she been more spirited, perhaps her husband would not have forsaken her;—men enlisted under the matrimonial banner, like those under the king's, would be often tempted to run away from their colours, if fear did not keep them in dread of desertion.

INIS

If making a husband afraid is the way to keep him faithful, I believe your lady will be the happiest wife in Spain.

MINETTE

Ha! ha! ha! how people may be deceived!—nay, how people are deceived!—but time will discover all things.

INIS

What! what, is there a secret in the business, Minette? if there is, hang time! let's have it directly.

MINETTE

Now, if I dared but tell ye—lud! lud! how I could surprise ye!—

[Going.]

INIS [Stopping her.]
Don't go.

MINETTE

I must go; I am on the very brink of betraying my mistress,—I must leave you—mercy upon me!—it rises like new bread.

INIS

I hope it will choke ye, if you stir till I know all.

MINETTE

Will you never breathe a syllable?

INIS

Never.

MINETTE

Will you strive to forget it the moment you have heard it?

INIS

I'll swear to myself forty times a-day to forget it.

MINETTE

You are sure you will not let me stir from this spot till you know the whole?

INIS

Not as far as a thrush hops.

MINETTE

So! now, then, in one word,—here it goes. Though every body supposes my lady an arrant scold, she's no more a—[Looking out.] Don Cæsar. [Without, L.] Out upon't e—h—h!

MINETTE

Oh, St. Gerome!—here is her father, and his privy counsellor, Gasper. I can never communicate a secret in quiet. Well! come to my chamber, for, now my hand's in, you shall have the whole.—I would not keep it another day to be confidant to an infanta.

[Exeunt, R.

[Enter **DON CAESAR** and **GASPER**, L.

GASPER

Take comfort, sir; take comfort.

DON CAESAR

Take it;—why, where the devil shall I find it? You may say, take physic, sir, or, take poison, sir—they are to be had; but what signifies bidding me take comfort, when I can neither buy it, beg it, nor steal it?

GASPER

But patience will bring it, sir.

DON CAESAR

'Tis false, sirrah.—Patience is a cheat, and the man that ranked her with the cardinal virtues was a fool. I have had patience at bed and board these three long years, but the comfort she promised, has never called in with a civil how d'ye?

GASPER

Ay, sir, but you know the poets say that the twin sister and companion of comfort is good humour. Now if you would but drop that agreeable acidity, which is so conspicuous—

DON CAESAR

Then let my daughter drop her perverse humour; 'tis a more certain bar to marriage than ugliness or folly; and will send me to my grave, at last, without male heirs. [Crying.] How many have laid siege to her! But that humour of hers, like the works of Gibraltar, no Spaniard can find pregnable.

GASPER

Ay, well—Troy held out but ten years—Let her once tell over her beads, unmarried at five-and-twenty, and, my life upon it, she ends the rosary, with a hearty prayer for a good husband.

DON CAESAR

What, d'ye expect me to wait till the horrors of old maidenism frighten her into civility? no, no;—I'll shut her up in a convent, marry myself, and have heirs in spite of her. There's my neighbour Don Vasquez's daughter, she is but nineteen—

GASPER

The very step I was going to recommend, sir. You are but a young gentleman of sixty-three, I take it; and a husband of sixty-three, who marries a wife of nineteen, will never want heirs, take my word for it.

DON CAESAR
What! do you joke, sirrah?

GASPER
Oh no, sir—not if you are serious. I think it would be one of the pleasantest things in the world—Madam would throw a new life into the family; and when you are above stairs in the gout, sir, the music of her concerts, and the spirit of her converzationes, would reach your sick bed, and be a thousand times more comforting than flannels and panada.

DON CAESAR
Come, come, I understand ye.—But this daughter of mine—I shall give her but two chances more.—Don Garcia and Don Vincentio will both be here to-day, and if she plays over the old game, I'll marry to-morrow morning, if I hang myself the next.

GASPER
You decide right, signor; at sixty-three the marriage noose and the hempen noose should always go together.

DON CAESAR
Why, you dog you, do you suppose—There's Don Garcia—there he is coming through the portico. Run to my daughter, and bid her remember what I have said to her.

[Exit **GASPER**, R.]

She has had her lesson—but another memento mayn't be amiss—a young slut! pretty, and witty, and rich—a match for a prince, and yet—but hist!—Not a word to my young man; if I can but keep him in ignorance till he is married, he must make the best of his bargain afterwards, as other honest men have done before him.

[Enter **GARCIA**, L.

Welcome, Don Garcia! why, you are rather before your time.

GARCIA
Gallantry forbid that I should not, when a fair lady is concerned. Should Donna Olivia welcome me as frankly as you do, I shall think I have been tardy.

DON CAESAR
When you made your overtures, signor, I understood it was from inclination to be allied to my family, not from a particular passion to my daughter. Have you ever seen her?

GARCIA
But once—that transiently—yet sufficient to convince me that she is charming.

DON CAESAR

Why, yes, though I say it, there are few prettier women in Madrid; and she has got enemies amongst her own sex accordingly. They pretend to say that—I say, sir, they have reported that she is not blessed with that kind of docility and gentleness that a—now, though she may not be so very placid, and insipid, as some young women, yet, upon the whole—

GARCIA
Oh, fie, sir!—not a word—a beauty cannot be ill-tempered; gratified vanity keeps her in good humour with herself, and every body about her.

DON CAESAR
Yes, as you say—vanity is a prodigious sweetener; and Olivia, considering how much she has been humoured, is as gentle and pliant as—

[Enter **MINETTE**, R.

MINETTE
Oh, sir! shield me from my mistress—She is in one of her old tempers—the whole house is in an uproar.—I cannot support it!

DON CAESAR
Hush!

MINETTE
No, sir, I can't hush—a saint could not bear it. I am tired of her tyranny, and must quit her service.

DON CAESAR
Then quit it in a moment—go to my steward, and receive your wages—go—begone. 'Tis a cousin of my daughter's she is speaking of.

MINETTE
A cousin, sir!—No, 'tis Donna Olivia, your daughter—my mistress. Oh, sir! you seem to be a sweet, tender-hearted young gentleman—'twould move you to pity if—[To **GARCIA**.]

DON CAESAR
I'll move you, hussy, to some purpose, if you don't move off.

GARCIA
I am really confounded—can the charming Olivia—

DON CAESAR
Spite, sir—mere malice! my daughter has refused her some cast gown, or some—

OLIVIA [Without, R.]
Where is she?—Where is Minette?

DON CAESAR
Oh, 'tis all over!—the tempest is coming.

[Enter **OLIVIA**, R.

OLIVIA
Oh, you vile creature!—to speak to me!—to answer me!—am I made to be answered?

DON CAESAR
Daughter! daughter!

OLIVIA
Because I threw my work-bag at her, she had the insolence to complain; and, on my repeating it, said she would not bear it.—Servants choose what they shall bear!

MINETTE
When you are married, ma'am, I hope your husband will bear your humour less patiently than I have done.

OLIVIA
My husband!—dost think my husband shall contradict my will? Oh, I long to set a pattern to those milky wives, whose mean compliances degrade the sex.

GARCIA
Opportune! [Aside.]

OLIVIA
The only husband on record who knew how to treat a wife was Socrates; and though his lady was a Grecian, I have some reason to believe her descendants matched into our family; and never shall my tame submission disgrace my ancestry.

GARCIA
Heavens! why have you never curbed this intemperate spirit, Don Caesar? [R. of **OLIVIA**.]

OLIVIA [Starting.]
Curbed, sir! talk thus to your groom—curbs and bridles for a woman's tongue!

GARCIA
Not for yours, lady, truly! 'tis too late. But had the torrent, not so overbearing, been taken at its spring, it might have been stemmed, and turned in gentle streamlets at the master's pleasure.

OLIVIA
A mistake, friend!—my spirit, at its spring, was too powerful for any master.

GARCIA
Indeed!—perhaps you may meet a Petruchio, gentle Catherine, yet.

OLIVIA
But no gentle Catherine will he find me, believe it.—Catherine! why, she had not the spirit of a roasted chestnut—a few big words, an empty oath, and a scanty dinner, made her as submissive as a spaniel. My fire will not be so soon extinguished—it shall resist big words, oaths, and starving.

MINETTE

I believe so, indeed; help the poor gentleman, I say, to whose fate you fall! [Returns up.]

GARCIA

Don Cæsar, adieu! My commiseration for your fate subdues the resentment I should otherwise feel at your endeavouring to deceive me into such a marriage. [Crosses, L.]

OLIVIA

Marriage! oh, mercy!—Is this Don Garcia! [Apart to **DON CAESAR**.]

DON CAESAR

Yes, termagant!

OLIVIA

O, what a misfortune! Why did you not tell me it was the gentleman you designed to marry me to?—Oh, sir! all that is past was in sport; a contrivance between my maid and me: I have no spirit at all—I am as patient as poverty.

GARCIA

This mask fits too ill on your features, fair lady: I have seen you without disguise, and rejoice in your ignorance of my name, since, but for that, my peaceful home might have become the seat of perpetual discord.

MINETTE

Ay, sir, you would never have known what a quiet hour—
[On R. of **OLIVIA**.]

OLIVIA [Strikes her.]

Impertinence! Indeed, sir, I can be as gentle and forbearing as a pet lamb.

GARCIA

I cannot doubt it, madam; the proofs of your placidity are very striking—But adieu! though I shall pray for your conversion, rather than have the honour of it—I'd turn Dominican, and condemn myself to perpetual celibacy.

[Exit, L.

DON CAESAR

Now, hussy!—now, hussy!—what do you expect?

OLIVIA

Dear me! how can you be so unreasonable! did ever daughter do more to oblige a father! I absolutely begged the man to have me.

DON CAESAR

Yes, vixen! after you had made him detest ye; what, I suppose, he did not hit your fancy, madam; though there is not, in all Spain, a man of prettier conversation.

OLIVIA

Yes he has a very pretty kind of conversation; 'tis like a parenthesis.

DON CAESAR

Like a parenthesis!

OLIVIA

Yes, it might be all left out, and never missed. However, I thought him a modest kind of a well-meaning young man, and that he would make a pretty sort of a husband—for notwithstanding his blustering, had I been his wife, in three months he should have been as humble and complaisant as—

DON CAESAR

Ay, there it is—there it is!—that spirit of yours, hussy, you can neither conquer nor conceal; but I'll find a way to tame it, I'll warrant me.

[Exit, R. **OLIVIA** and **MINETTE** follow him with their eyes, and then burst into a laugh.

MINETTE

Well, madam, I give you joy! had other ladies as much success in getting lovers, as you have in getting rid of yours, what contented faces we should see!

OLIVIA

But to what purpose do I get rid of them, whilst they rise in succession like monthly pinks? Was there ever any thing so provoking? After some quiet, and believing the men had ceased to trouble themselves about me, no less than two proposals have been made to my inexorable father this very day—What will become of me?

MINETTE

What should become of you? You'll chuse one from the pair, I hope. Believe me, madam, the only way to get rid of the impertinence of lovers, is to take one, and make him a scarecrow to the rest.

OLIVIA

Oh, but I cannot!—Invention assist me this one day!

MINETTE

Upon my word, madam, invention owes you nothing; and I am afraid you can draw on that bank no longer.—You must trust to your established character of vixen.

OLIVIA

But that won't frighten them all, you know, though it did its business with sober Don Garcia. The brave General Antonio would have made a property of me, in spite of every thing, had I not luckily discovered his antipathy to cats, and so scared the hero, by pretending an immoderate passion for young kittens.

MINETTE

Yes, but you was still harder pushed by the Castilian Count, and his engraved genealogy from Noah.

OLIVIA

Oh, he would have kept his post as immovably as the griffins at his gate, had I not very seriously imparted to him, that my mother's great uncle sold oranges in Arragon.

MINETTE
And pray, madam, if I may be so bold, who is the next gentleman?

OLIVIA
Oh, Don Vincentio, who distracts every body with his skill in music. He ought to be married to a Viol de Gamba. I bless my stars I have never yet had a miser in my list—on such a character all art would be lost, and nothing but an earthquake, to swallow up my estate, could save me.

MINETTE
Well, if some one did but know, how happy would some one be, that for his sake—

OLIVIA
Now, don't be impertinent, Minette. You have several times attempted to slide yourself into a secret, which I am resolved to keep to myself. Continue faithful, and suppress your curiosity.

[Exit, R.

MINETTE
Suppress my curiosity, madam!—why, I am a chambermaid, and a sorry one too, it should seem, to have been in your confidence two years, and never have got the master-secret yet. I never was six weeks in a family before, but I knew every secret they had in it for three generations; ay, and I'll know this too, or I'll blow up all her plans, and declare to the world, that she is no more a vixen than other fine ladies—they have most of them a touch on't.

[Exit, R.

ACT II

SCENE I.—An Apartment at Donna Laura's

Enter **LAURA**, followed by **CARLOS**, L.

CARLOS
Nay, madam, you may as well stop here, for I'll follow you through every apartment, but I will be heard.

[Seizing her hand.]

LAURA
This insolence is not to be endured; within my own walls to be thus—

CARLOS
The time has been, when within your walls I might be master.

LAURA

Yes, you were then master of my heart; that gave you a right which—

CARLOS

You have now transferred to another.

[Flinging away her hand.]

LAURA

Well, sir!

CARLOS

"Well, sir!"—Unblushing acknowledgement! False, fickle woman!

LAURA

Because I have luckily got the start of you; in a few weeks I should have been the accuser, and you the false and fickle.

CARLOS

And to secure yourself from that disgrace, you prudently looked out in time for another lover.

LAURA

I can pardon your sneer, because you are mortified.

CARLOS

Mortified!

LAURA

Yes, mortified to the soul, Carlos!

CARLOS [Stamping.]

Madam! madam!

LAURA

This rage would have been all cool insolence had I waited for your change—Scarcely would you have deigned to form a phrase of pity for me; perhaps have bid me forget a man no longer worthy my attachment, and recommended me to hartshorn and my women.

CARLOS

Has any hour, since I have first known you, given you cause for such unjust—

LAURA

Yes, every hour—Now, Carlos I bring thee to the test!—You saw, you liked, you loved me; was there no fond trusting woman whom you deserted, to indulge the transient passion? Yes, one blessed with beauty, gentleness, and youth; one, who more than her own being loved thee, who made thee rich, and whom thou madest thy wife.

CARLOS

My wife!—here's a turn! So to revenge the quarrels of my wife—

LAURA

No, do not mistake me—what I have done was merely to indulge myself, without more regard to your feelings, than you had to hers.

CARLOS

And you dare avow to my face, that you have a passion for another?

LAURA

I do, and—for I am above disguise, I confess, so tender is my love for Florio, it has scarcely left a trace of that I once avowed for Carlos.

CARLOS

Well, madam, if I hear this without some sudden vengeance on the tongue which speaks it, thank the annihilation of that passion, whose remembrance is as dead in my bosom as in yours. Let us, however, part friends, and with a mutual acquittal of every obligation—so give up the settlement of that estate, which left me almost a beggar.

LAURA

Give it up!—ha! ha!—no, Carlos, you consigned me that estate as a proof of love; do not imagine, then, I'll give up the only part of our connexion of which I am not ashamed.

CARLOS

Base woman! you know it was not a voluntary gift—after having in vain practised on my fondness, whilst in a state of intoxication, you prevailed on me to sign the deed, which you had artfully prepared for the purpose—therefore you must restore it.

LAURA

Never, never.

CARLOS

Ruin is in the word!—Call it back, madam, or I'll be revenged on thee in thy heart's dearest object—thy minion, Florio!—he shall not riot on my fortune.

LAURA

Ha! ha! ha! Florio is safe—your lands are sold, and in another country we shall enjoy the blessing of thy fond passion, whilst that passion is indulging itself in hatred and execrations.

[Exit, R.

CARLOS

My vengeance shall first fall on her. [Following.] No, he shall be the first victim, or 'twill be incomplete.—Reduced to poverty, I cannot live;—Oh, folly! where are now all the gilded prospects of my youth? Had I—but 'tis too late to look back,—remorse attends the past, and ruin—ruin waits me in the future!

[Exit, L.

SCENE II.—Don Caesar's

VICTORIA enters L., perusing a letter; enter OLIVIA, R.

OLIVIA [Speaks as entering.]
If my father should inquire for me, tell him I am in Donna Victoria's apartment.—Smiling, I protest! my dear gloomy cousin, where have you purchased that sun-shiny look?

VICTORIA
It is but April sunshine, I fear; but who could resist such a temptation to smile? a letter from Donna Laura, my husband's mistress, styling me her dearest Florio! her life! her soul! and complaining of a twelve hours absence, as the bitterest misfortune.

OLIVIA
Ha! ha! ha! most doughty Don! pray, let us see you in your feather and doublet; as a Cavaleiro, it seems, you are formidable. So suddenly to rob your husband of his charmer's heart! you must have used some witchery.

VICTORIA
Yes, powerful witchery—the knowledge of my sex. Oh! did the men but know us, as well as we do ourselves;—but, thank fate they do not—'twould be dangerous.

OLIVIA
What, I suppose, you praised her understanding, was captivated by her wit, and absolutely struck dumb by the amazing beauties of—her mind.

VICTORIA
Oh, no,—that's the mode prescribed by the essayists on the female heart—ha! ha! ha!—Not a woman breathing, from fifteen to fifty, but would rather have a compliment to the tip of her ear, or the turn of her ancle, than a volume in praise of her intellects.

OLIVIA
So, flattery, then, is your boasted pill?

VICTORIA
No, that's only the occasional gilding; but 'tis in vain to attempt a description of what changed its nature with every moment. I was now attentive—now gay—then tender, then careless. I strove rather to convince her that I was charming, than that I myself was charmed; and when I saw love's arrow quivering in her heart, instead of falling at her feet, sung a triumphant air, and remembered a sudden engagement.

OLIVIA [Archly.]
Would you have done so, had you been a man?

VICTORIA

Assuredly—knowing what I now do as a woman.

OLIVIA

But can all this be worth while, merely to rival a fickle husband with one woman, whilst he is setting his feather, perhaps, at half a score others?

VICTORIA

To rival him was not my first motive. The Portuguese robbed me of his heart; I concluded she had fascinations which nature had denied to me; it was impossible to visit her as a woman; I, therefore, assumed the Cavalier, to study her, that I might, if possible, be to my Carlos, all he found in her.

OLIVIA

Pretty humble creature?

VICTORIA

In this adventure I learnt more than I expected;—my (oh, cruel!) my husband has given this woman an estate, almost all that his dissipations had left us.

OLIVIA

Indeed!

VICTORIA

To make him more culpable, it was my estate; it was that fortune which my lavish love had made his, without securing it to my children.

OLIVIA

How could you be so improvident?

VICTORIA

Alas! I trusted him with my heart, with my happiness, without restriction. Should I have shown a greater solicitude for any thing, than for these?

OLIVIA

The event proves that you should; but how can you be thus passive in your sorrow? since I had assumed the man, I'd make him feel a man's resentment for such injuries.

VICTORIA

Oh, Olivia! what resentment can I show to him I have vowed to honour, and whom, both my duty and my heart compel me yet to love.

OLIVIA

Why, really now, I think—positively, there's no thinking about it; 'tis among the arcana of the married life, I suppose.

VICTORIA

You, who know me, can judge how I suffered in prosecuting my plan. I have thrown off the delicacy of sex; I have worn the mask of love to the destroyer of my peace—but the object is too great to be abandoned—nothing less than to save my husband from ruin, and to restore him, again a lover, to my faithful bosom.

OLIVIA

Well, I confess, Victoria, I hardly know whether most to blame or praise you; but, with the rest of the world, I suppose, your success will determine me.

[Enter **GASPER**, L.

GASPER

Pray, madam, are your wedding shoes ready? [To **OLIVIA**.]

OLIVIA

Insolence!—I can scarcely ever keep up the vixen to this fellow. [Apart to **VICTORIA**.]

GASPER

You'll want them, ma'am, to-morrow morning, that's all—so I came to prepare ye.

OLIVIA

I want wedding shoes to-morrow! if you are kept on water gruel till I marry, that plump face of yours will be chap-fallen, I believe.

GASPER

Yes, truly, I believe so too. Lackaday, did you suppose I came to bring you news of your own wedding? no such glad tidings for you, lady, believe me.—You married! I am sure the man who ties himself to you, ought to be half a salamander, and able to live in fire.

OLIVIA

What marriage, then, is it, you do me the honour to inform me of?

GASPER

Why, your father's marriage. You'll have a mother-in-law to-morrow, and having, like a dutiful daughter, danced at the wedding, be immured in a convent for life.

OLIVIA

Immured in a convent! then I'll raise sedition in the sisterhood, depose the abbess, and turn the confessor's chair to a go-cart.

GASPER

So, the threat of the mother-in-law, which I thought would be worse than that of the abbess, does not frighten ye?

OLIVIA

No, because my father dares not give me one.—Marry, without my consent! no, no, he'll never think of it, depend on't; however, lest the fit should grow strong upon him, I'll go and administer my volatiles to keep it under.

[Exit L. H.]

GASPER

Administer them cautiously then: too strong a dose of your volatiles would make the fit stubborn. Who'd think that pretty arch look belonged to a termagant? what a pity! 'twould be worth a thousand ducats to cure her.

VICTORIA

Has Inis told you I wanted to converse with you in private, Gasper?

GASPER

Oh, yes, madam, and I took particular notice, that it was to be in private.—Sure, says I, Mrs. Inis, Madam Victoria has not taken a fancy to me, and is going to break her mind.

VICTORIA

Whimsical! ha! ha! suppose I should, Gasper?

GASPER

Why, then, madam, I should say, fortune had used you devilish scurvily, to give you a gray-beard in a livery. I know well enough, that some young ladies have given themselves to gray-beards, in a gilded coach, and others have run away with a handsome youth in worsted lace; they each had their apology; but if you run away with me—pardon me, madam, I could not stand the ridicule.

VICTORIA

Oh, very well; but if you refuse to run away with me, will you do me another favour?

GASPER

Any thing you'll order, madam, except dancing a fandango.

VICTORIA

You have seen my rich old uncle in the country?

GASPER

What, Don Sancho, who, with two thirds of a century in his face, affects the misdemeanors of youth; hides his baldness with amber locks, and complains of the tooth-ache, to make you believe, that the two rows of ivory he carries in his head, grew there?

VICTORIA

Oh, you know him, I find; could you assume his character for an hour, and make love for him? you know, it must be in the style of King Roderigo the First.

GASPER

Hang it! I am rather too near his own age; to appear an old man with effect, one should not be above twenty; 'tis always so on the stage.

VICTORIA

Pho! you might pass for Juan's grandson.

GASPER

Nay, if your ladyship condesends to flatter me, you have me.

VICTORIA
Then follow me; for Don Cæsar, I hear, is approaching—in the garden I'll make you acquainted with my plan, and impress on your mind every trait of my uncle's character. If you can hit him off, the arts of Laura shall be foiled, and Carlos be again Victoria's.

[Exeunt, R.

[Enter **DON CAESAR**, followed by **OLIVIA**, L.

DON CAESAR
No, no, 'tis too late—no coaxings; I am resolved, I say.

OLIVIA
But it is not too late, and you shan't be resolved, I say. Indeed, now, I'll be upon my guard with the next Don—what's his name? not a trace of the Xantippe left.—I'll study to be charming.

DON CAESAR
Nay, you need not study it, you are always charming enough, if you would but hold your tongue.

OLIVIA
Do you think so? then to the next lover I won't open my lips; I'll answer every thing he says with a smile, and if he asks me to have him, drop a courtesy of thankfulness.

DON CAESAR
Pshaw! that's too much t'other way; you are always either above the mark or below it; you must talk, but talk with good humour. Can't you look gently and prettily, now, as I do? and say, yes, sir, and no, sir; and 'tis very fine weather, sir; and pray, sir, were you at the ball last night? and, I caught a sad cold the other evening; and bless me! I hear Lucinda has run away with her footman, and Don Philip has married his housemaid?—That's the way agreeable ladies talk; you never hear any thing else.

OLIVIA
Very true; and you shall see me as agreeable as the best of them, if you won't give me a mother-in-law to snub me, and set me tasks, and to take up all the fine apartments, and send up poor little Livy to lodge next the stars.

DON CAESAR
Ha! if thou wert but always thus soft and good-humoured, no mother-in-law in Spain, though she brought the Castiles for her portion, should have power to snub thee. But, Livy, the trial's at hand, for at this moment do I expect Don Vincentio to visit you. He is but just returned from England, and, probably, has yet heard only of your beauty and fortune; I hope it is not from you he will learn the other part of your character.

OLIVIA
This moment expect him! two new lovers in a day?

DON CAESAR

Beginning already, as I hope to live! ay, I see 'tis in vain; I'll send him an excuse, and marry Marcella before night.

OLIVIA

Oh, no! upon my obedience, I promise to be just the soft, civil creature, you have described.

[Enter a **SERVANT**, L.

SERVANT

Don Vincentio is below, sir.

[Exit, L.

DON CAESAR

I'll wait upon him—well, go and collect all your smiles and your simpers, and remember all I have said to you;—be gentle, and talk pretty little small talk, d'ye hear, and if you please him, you shall have the portion of a Dutch burgomaster's daughter, and the pin-money of a princess, you jade, you. I think at last, I have done it; the fear of this mother-in-law will keep down the fiend in her, if any thing can.

[Exit, L.

OLIVIA

Hah! my poor father, your anxieties will never end till you bring Don Julio. But what shall I do with this Vincentio?—I fear he is so perfectly harmonized, that to put him in an ill temper will be impracticable.—I must try, however; if 'tis possible to find a discord in him, I'll touch the string.

[Exit, R.

SCENE III.—Another Apartment

Enter **DON CAESAR** and **VINCENTIO**, L.

VINCENTIO

Presto, presto, signior! where is the Olivia?—not a moment to spare. I left off in all the fury of composition; minums and crotchets have been battling it through my head the whole day, and trying a semibreve in G sharp, has made me as flat as double F.

DON CAESAR

Sharp and flat!—trying a semibreve!—oh—gad, sir! I had like not to have understood you; but a semibreve is something of a demi-culverin, I take it; and you have been practising the art military.

VINCENTIO

Art military!—what, sir! are you unacquainted with music?

DON CAESAR

Music! oh, I ask pardon: then you are fond of music—'ware of discords! [Aside.]

VINCENTIO

Fond of it! devoted to it.—I composed a thing to-day, in all the gusto of Sacchini, and the sweetness of Gluck. But this recreant finger fails me in composing a passage in E octave; if it does not gain more elastic vigour in a week, I shall be tempted to have it amputated, and supply the shake with a spring.

DON CAESAR

Mercy! amputate a finger, to supply a shake!

VINCENTIO

Oh, that's a trifle in the road to reputation—to be talked of, is the summum bonum of this life.—A young man of rank should not glide through the world, without a distinguished rage, or, as they call it in England—a hobby-horse.

DON CAESAR

A hobby horse!

VINCENTIO

Yes; that is, every man of figure determines on setting out in life, in that land of liberty, in what line to ruin himself; and that choice is called his hobby-horse. One makes the turf his scene of action—another drives about tall phaetons, to peep into their neighbour's garret windows; and a third rides his hobby-horse in parliament, where it jerks him sometimes on one side, and sometimes on the other; sometimes in, and sometimes out; till at length, he is jerked out of his honesty, and his constituents out of their freedom.

DON CAESAR

Ay! Well, 'tis a wonder, that with such sort of hobby-horses as these, they should still outride all the world, to the goal of glory.

VINCENTIO

This is all cantabile; nothing to do with the subject of the piece, which is Donna Olivia;—pray give me the key note to her heart.

DON CAESAR

Upon my word, signor, to speak in your own phrase, I believe that note has never yet been sounded.—Ah! here she comes! look at her.—Isn't she a fine girl?

VINCENTIO

Touching! Musical, I'll be sworn! her very air is harmonious!

DON CAESAR [Aside.]

I wish thou may'st find her tongue so.

[Enter **OLIVIA**, courtesies profoundly to each. R.

Daughter, receive Don Vincentio—his rank, fortune, and merit, entitle him to the heiress of a grandee; but he is contented to become my son-in-law, if you can please him.

[Crosses, R. **OLIVIA** courtesies again.

VINCENTIO

Please me! she entrances me! Her presence thrills me like a cadenza of Pachierotti's, and every nerve vibrates to the music of her looks.

Her step andante gently moves,
Pianos glance from either eye;
Oh how larghetto is the heart,
That charms so forté can defy!

Donna Olivia, will you be contented to receive me as a lover?

OLIVIA

Yes, sir—No, sir.

VINCENTIO

Yes, sir! no, sir! bewitching timidity?

DON CAESAR

Yes, sir, she's remarkably timid,—She's in the right cue, I see. [Aside.]

VINCENTIO

'Tis clear you have never travelled.—I shall be delighted to show you England.—You will there see how entirely timidity is banished the sex. You must affect a marked character, and maintain it at all hazards.

OLIVIA

'Tis a very fine day, sir.

VINCENTIO

Madam!

OLIVIA

I caught a sad cold the other evening.—Pray, was you at the ball last night?

VINCENTIO

What ball, fair lady?

OLIVIA

Bless me! they say, Lucinda has run away with her footman, and Don Philip has married his house-maid. Now, am I not very agreeable? [Apart to **DON CAESAR**.]

DON CAESAR

O, such perverse obedience!

VINCENTIO

Really, madam, I have not the honour to know Don Philip and Lucinda—nor am I happy enough, entirely to comprehend you.

OLIVIA

No! I only meant to be agreeable—but, perhaps, you have no taste for pretty little small talk!

VINCENTIO

Pretty little small talk!

OLIVIA

A marked character you admire; so do I, I dote on it.—I would not resemble the rest of the world in any thing.

VINCENTIO

My taste to the fiftieth part of a crotchet!—We shall agree admirably when we are married!

OLIVIA

And that will be unlike the rest of the world, and therefore, charming!

DON CAESAR [Aside.]

It will do! I have hit her humour at last. Why didn't this young dog offer himself before?

OLIVIA

I believe, I have the honour to carry my taste that way, farther than you, Don Vincentio. Pray, now, what is your usual style in living?

VINCENTIO

My winters I spend in Madrid, as other people do. My summers I drawl through at my castle—

OLIVIA

As other people do!—and yet you pretend to taste and singularity, ha! ha! ha! Good Don Vincentio, never talk of a marked character again. Go into the country in July, to smell roses and woodbines, when every body regales on their fragrance! Now, I would rusticate only in winter, and my bleak castle should be decorated with verdure and flowers, amidst the soft zephyrs of December.

DON CAESAR [Aside.]

Oh, she'll go too far!

OLIVIA

On the leafless trees I would hang green branches—the labour of silk worms, and therefore, natural; whilst my rose shrubs and myrtles should be scented by the first perfumers in Italy. Unnatural, indeed, but, therefore, singular and striking.

VINCENTIO

Oh, charming! You beat me, where I thought myself the strongest. Would they but establish newspapers here, to paragraph our singularities, we should be the most envied couple in Spain!

DON CAESAR [Aside.]

By St. Antony, he is as mad as she is!

VINCENTIO

What say you, Don Cæsar? Olivia, and her winter garden, and I and my music.

OLIVIA

Music, did you say? Music! I am passionately fond of that!

DON CAESAR

She has saved my life! I thought she was going to knock down his hobby-horse. [Aside.]

VINCENTIO

You enchant me! I have the finest band in Madrid—My first violin draws a longer bow than Giardini; my clarionets, my viol de gamba—Oh, you shall have such concerts!

OLIVIA

Concerts! Pardon me there—My passion is a single instrument.

VINCENTIO

That's carrying singularity very far indeed! I love a crash; so does every body of taste.

OLIVIA

But my taste isn't like every body's; my nerves are so particularly fine, that more than one instrument overpowers them.

VINCENTIO

Pray tell me the name of that one: I am sure it must be the most elegant and captivating in the world.—I am impatient to know it.—We'll have no other instrument in Spain, and I will study to become its master, that I may woo you with its music. Charming Olivia! tell me, is it a harpsichord? a piano forte? a pentachord? a harp?

OLIVIA

You have it, you have it; a harp—yes, a Jew's-harp is, to me, the only instrument. Are you not charmed with the delightful h—u—m of its base, running on the ear, like the distant rumble of a state coach? It presents the idea of vastness and importance to the mind. The moment you are its master—I'll give you my hand.

VINCENTIO

Da capo, madam, da capo! a Jew's-harp!

OLIVIA

Bless me, sir, don't I tell you so? Violins chill me; clarionets, by sympathy, hurt my lungs; and, instead of maintaining a band under my roof, I would not keep a servant, who knew a bassoon from a flute, or could tell whether he heard a jigg, or a canzonetta.

DON CAESAR

Oh thou perverse one! you know you love concerts—you know you do. [In great agitation.]

OLIVIA

I detest them! It's vulgar custom that attaches people to the sound of fifty different instruments at once; 'twould be as well to talk on the same subject, in fifty different tongues. A band; 'tis a mere olio of sound! I'd rather listen to a three-stringed guitar serenading a sempstress in some neighbouring garret.

DON CAESAR
Oh you—Don Vincentio, [Crosses, C.] this is nothing but perverseness, wicked perverseness. Hussy!—didn't you shake, when you mentioned a garret? didn't bread and water, and a step-mother, come into your head at the same time?

VINCENTIO
Piano, piano, good sir! Spare yourself all farther trouble. Should the Princess of Guzzarat, and all her diamond mines, offer themselves, I would not accept them, in lieu of my band—a band, that has half ruined me to collect. I would have allowed Donna Olivia a blooming garden in winter; I would even have procured barrenness and snow for her in the dog-days; but, to have my band insulted!—to have my knowledge in music slighted!—to be roused from all the energies of composition, by the drone of a Jew's-harp, I cannot breathe under the idea.

DON CAESAR
Then—then you refuse her, sir!

VINCENTIO
I cannot use so harsh a word—I take my leave of the lady.—Adieu, madam—I leave you to enjoy your solos, whilst I fly to the raptures of a crash.

[Exit, L.

[**DON CAESAR** goes up to her, and looks her in the face; then goes off without speaking, L.

OLIVIA
Mercy; that silent anger is terrifying: I read a young mother-in-law, and an old lady abbess, in every line of his face.

[Enter **VICTORIA**, R.

Well, you heard the whole, I suppose—heard poor unhappy me scorned and rejected.

VICTORIA
I heard you in imminent danger; and expected Signor Da Capo would have snapped you up, in spite of caprice and extravagance.

OLIVIA
Oh, they charmed, instead of scaring him. I soon found, that my only chance was to fall across his caprice. Where is the philosopher who could withstand that?

VICTORIA
But what, my good cousin, does all this tend to?

OLIVIA

I dare say you can guess. Penelope had never cheated her lovers with a never-ending web, had she not had an Ulysses.

VICTORIA
An Ulysses! what, are you then married?

OLIVIA
O no, not yet! but, believe me, my design is not to lead apes; nor is my heart an icicle. If you choose to know more, put on your veil, and slip with me through the garden, to the Prado.

VICTORIA
I can't, indeed. I am this moment going to dress en homme to visit the impatient Portuguese.

OLIVIA
Send an excuse; for, positively, you go with me. Heaven and earth! I am going to meet a man! whom I have been fool enough, to dream and think of these two years, and I don't know that ever he thought of me in his life.

VICTORIA
Two years discovering that?

OLIVIA
He has been abroad. The only time I ever saw him was at the Duchess of Medina's—there were a thousand people; and he was so elegant, so careless, so handsome!—In a word, though he set off for France the next morning, by some witchcraft or other, he has been before my eyes ever since.

VICTORIA
Was the impression mutual?

OLIVIA
He hardly noticed me. I was then a bashful thing just out of a convent, and shrunk from observation.

VICTORIA
Why, I thought you were going to meet him.

OLIVIA
To be sure; I sent him a command this morning, to be at the Prado. I am determined to find out if his heart is engaged, and if it is—

VICTORIA
You'll cross your arms, and crown your brow with willows?

OLIVIA
No, positively; not whilst we have myrtles. I would prefer Julio, 'tis true, to all his sex; but if he is stupid enough to be insensible to me, I shan't for that reason, pine like a girl, on chalk and oatmeal.—No, no; in that case, I shall form a new plan, and treat my future lovers with more civility.

VICTORIA

You are the only woman in love, I ever heard talk reasonably.

OLIVIA
Well, prepare for the Prado, and I'll give you a lesson against your days of widowhood. Don't you wish this the moment, Victoria? A pretty widow at four-and-twenty has more subjects, and a wider empire, than the first monarch upon earth. I long to see you in your weeds.

VICTORIA
Never may you see them! Oh, Olivia! my happiness, my life, depend on my husband. The fond hope of still being united to him, gives me spirits in my affliction, and enables me to support even the period of his neglect with patience.

[Exeunt, R.

ACT III

SCENE I.—A Long Street

JULIO enters from a Garden Gate in flat, with precipitation; a **SERVANT**, within, fastens the Gate.

JULIO
Yes, yes, bar the gate fast, Cerberus, lest some other curious traveller should stumble on your confines.—If ever I am so caught again—

GARCIA enters L.; going hastily across, **JULIO** seizes him.

Don Garcia, never make love to a woman in a veil.

GARCIA
Why so, pr'ythee? Veils and secrecy are the chief ingredients in a Spanish amour; but in two years, Julio, thou art grown absolutely French.

JULIO
That may be; but if ever I trust to a veil again, may no lovely, blooming beauty ever trust me. Why dost know, I have been an hour at the feet of a creature, whose first birth-day must have been kept the latter end of the last century, and whose trembling, weak voice, I mistook for the timid cadence of bashful fifteen!

GARCIA
Ha! ha! ha! What a happiness to have seen thee in thy raptures, petitioning for half a glance only, of the charms the envious veil concealed!

JULIO
Yes; and when she unveiled her Gothic countenance, to render the thing completely ridiculous, she began moralizing; and positively would not let me out of the snare, till I had persuaded her she had worked a conversion, and that I'd never make love—but in an honest way, again.

GARCIA
Oh, that honest way of love-making is delightful, to be sure! I had a dose of it this morning; but, happily, the ladies have not yet learned to veil their tempers, though they have their faces.

[Enter **DON VINCENTIO**, R.

VINCENTIO
Julio! Garcia! congratulate me!—Such an escape!

[Crosses to C.

JULIO
What have you escaped?

VINCENTIO
Matrimony.

GARCIA
Nay, then our congratulations may be mutual. I have had a matrimonial escape too, this very day. I was almost on the brink of the ceremony with the veriest Xantippe!

VINCENTIO
Oh, that was not my case—mine was a sweet creature, all elegance, all life.

JULIO
Then where's the cause of congratulation?

VINCENTIO
Cause! why she's ignorant of music! prefers a jig to a canzonetta, and a Jew's-harp to a pentachord.

GARCIA
Had my nymph no other fault, I would pardon that, for she was lovely and rich.

VINCENTIO
Mine, too, was lovely and rich; and, I'll be sworn, as ignorant of scolding, as of the gamba!—but not to know music!

JULIO
Gentle, lovely, and rich! and ignorant only of music?

GARCIA
A venial crime indeed! if the sweet creature will marry me, she shall carry a Jew's-harp always in her train, as a Scotch laird does his bagpipes. I wish you'd give me your interest.

VINCENTIO
Oh, most willingly, if thou hast so gross an inclination; I'll name thee as a dull-souled, largo fellow, to her father, Don Cæsar.

GARCIA
Cæsar! what Don Cæsar?

VINCENTIO
De Zuniga.

GARCIA
Impossible!

VINCENTIO
Oh, I'll answer for her mother. So much is Don Zuniga, her father, that he does not know a semibreve from a culverin!

GARCIA
The name of the lady?

VINCENTIO
Olivia.

GARCIA
Why you must be mad—that's my termagant!

VINCENTIO
Termagant!—ha! ha! ha! Thou hast certainly some vixen of a mistress, who infects thy ears towards the whole sex. Olivia is timid and elegant.

GARCIA
By Juno, there never existed such a scold!

VINCENTIO
By Orpheus, there never was a gayer tempered creature!—Spirit enough to be charming, that's all. If she loved harmony, I'd marry her to-morrow.

JULIO
Ha! ha! what a ridiculous jangle! 'Tis evident you speak of two different women.

GARCIA
I speak of Donna Olivia, heiress to Don Cæsar de Zuniga.

VINCENTIO
I speak of the heiress of Don Cæsar de Zuniga, who is called Donna Olivia.

GARCIA
Sir, I perceive you mean to insult me.

VINCENTIO

Your perceptions are very rapid, sir, but if you choose to think so, I'll settle that point with you immediately: But for fear of consequences, I'll fly home, and add the last bar to my concerto, and then meet you where you please.

[Crosses, L.

JULIO
Pho! this is evidently misapprehension. [Crosses, C.] To clear the matter up, I'll visit the lady, if you'll introduce me, Vincentio;—but you shall both promise to be governed in this dispute, by my decision.

VINCENTIO
I'll introduce you with joy, if you'll try to persuade her of the necessity of music, and the charms of harmony.

GARCIA
Yes, she needs that—You'll find her all jar and discord.

JULIO
Come, no more, Garcia; thou art but a sort of male vixen thyself. Melodious Vincentio, when shall I expect you?

VINCENTIO
This evening.

JULIO
Not this evening; I have engaged to meet a goldfinch in a grove—then I shall have music, you rogue!

VINCENTIO
It won't sing at night.

JULIO
Then I'll talk to it till the morning, and hear it pour out its matins to the rising sun. Call on me to-morrow; I'll then attend you to Donna Olivia, and declare faithfully the impression her character makes on me.—Come, Garcia, I must not leave you together, lest his crotchets and your minums should fall into a crash of discords.

[Exeunt, **VINCENTIO**, L., **JULIO** and **GARCIA**, R.

SCENE II.—The Prado

Enter **DON CARLOS**, R.

CARLOS
All hail to the powers of burgundy! Three flasks to my own share! What sorrows can stand against three flasks of burgundy? I was a damned melancholy fellow this morning, going to shoot myself, to get rid of my troubles.—Where are my troubles now? Gone to the moon, to look for my wits; and there I hope

they'll remain together, if one cannot come back without t'other. But where is this indolent dog, Julio? He fit to receive appointments from ladies! Sure I have not missed the hour—No, but seven yet—[Looking at his watch.]—Seven's the hour, by all the joys of burgundy! The rogue must be here—let's reconnoitre.

[Retires, R.

[Enter **VICTORIA** and **OLIVIA**, veiled, L. U. E.

OLIVIA
Positively, mine's a pretty spark, to let me be first at the place of appointment. I have half resolved to go home again, to punish him.

VICTORIA
I'll answer for its being but half a resolution—to make it entire, would be to punish yourself.—There's a solitary man—is not that he?

OLIVIA
I think not. If he'd please to turn his face this way—

VICTORIA
That's impossible, while the loadstone is the other way. He is looking at the woman in the next walk. Can't you disturb him?

OLIVIA [Screams.]
Oh! a frightful frog!

[**CARLOS** turns on R.

VICTORIA
Heavens, 'tis my husband!

OLIVIA
Your husband! Is that Don Carlos?

VICTORIA
It is indeed.

OLIVIA
Why, really, now I see the man, I don't wonder that you are in no hurry for your weeds. He is moving towards us.

VICTORIA
I cannot speak to him, and yet my soul flies to meet him.

CARLOS
Pray, lady, what occasioned that pretty scream? I shrewdly suspect it was a trap.

OLIVIA

A trap! ha! ha! ha!—a trap for you!

CARLOS

Why not, madam? Zounds, a man near six feet high, and three flasks of burgundy in his head, is worth laying a trap for.

OLIVIA

Yes, unless he happens to be trapped before. 'Tis about two years since you was caught, I take it—do keep farther off!—Odious! A married man!

CARLOS

The devil! is it posted under every saint in the street, that I am a married man?

OLIVIA

No, you carry the marks about you; that rueful phiz could never belong to a bachelor. Besides, there's an odd appearance on your temples—does your hat sit easily?

CARLOS

By all the thorns of matrimony, if—

OLIVIA

Poor man! how natural to swear by what one feels—but why were you in such haste to gather the thorns of matrimony? Bless us! had you but looked about you a little, what a market might have been made of that fine, proper, promising person of yours.

CARLOS

Confound thee, confound thee! If thou art a wife, may thy husband plague thee with jealousies, and thou never be able to give him cause for them; and if thou art a maid, may'st thou be an old one!

[Going, R. meets **DON JULIO**.]

Oh, Julio, look not that way; there's a tongue will stun thee!

JULIO

Heaven be praised! I love female prattle. A woman's tongue can never scare me. Which of these two goldfinches makes the music?

CARLOS [Crosses to **VICTORIA**.]

Oh, this is as silent as a turtle—[Taking **VICTORIA'S** hand.]—only coos now and then,—Perhaps you don't hate a married man, sweet one?

VICTORIA

You guess right; I love a married man.

CARLOS

Hah, say'st thou so? wilt thou love me?

VICTORIA

Will you let me?

CARLOS

Let thee, my charmer! how I'll cherish thee for't. What would I not give for thy heart!

VICTORIA

I demand a price, that, perhaps, you cannot give—I ask unbounded love; but you have a wife.

CARLOS

And, therefore, the readier to love every other woman; 'tis in your favour, child.

VICTORIA

Will you love me ever?

CARLOS

Ever! yes, ever; till we find each other dull company, and yawn, and talk of our neighbours for amusement.

VICTORIA

Farewell! I suspected you to be a bad chapman, and that you would not reach my terms.

[Going.]

CARLOS

Nay, I'll come to your terms, if I can;—but move this way; [Crosses, L.] I am fearful of that woodpecker at your elbow—should she begin again, her noise will scare all the pretty loves that are playing about my heart. Don't turn your head towards them; if you like to listen to love tales, you'll meet fond pairs enough in this walk.

[Forcing her gently off.

JULIO

I really believe, though you deny it, that you are my destiny—that is, you fated me hither. See, is not this your mandate?

[Taking a letter from his pocket.

OLIVIA

Oh, delightful! the scrawl of some chambermaid: or, perhaps, of your valet, to give you an air. What is it signed? Marriatornes? Tomasa? Sancha?

JULIO

Nay, now I am convinced the letter is yours, since you abuse it: so you may as well confess?

OLIVIA

Suppose I should, you can't be sure that I do not deceive you.

JULIO

True; but there is one point in which I have made a vow not to be deceived; therefore, the preliminary is, that you throw off your veil.

OLIVIA

My veil!

JULIO

Positively! if you reject this article, our negotiation ends.

OLIVIA

You have no right to offer articles, unless you own yourself conquered.

JULIO

I own myself willing to be conquered, and have, therefore, a right to make the best terms I can. Do you accede to the demand?

OLIVIA

Certainly not.

JULIO

You had better.

OLIVIA

I protest I will not.

JULIO [Aside.]

My life upon't, I make you. Why, madam, how absurd this is!—yet, 'tis of no consequence, for I know your features, as well as though I saw them.

OLIVIA

How can that be?

JULIO

I judge of what you hide, by what I see—I could draw your picture.

OLIVIA

Charming! pray begin the portrait.

JULIO

Imprimis, a broad high forehead, rounded at the top, like an old-fashioned gateway.

OLIVIA

Oh, horrid!

JULIO

Little gray eyes, a sharp nose, and hair, the colour of rusty prunella.

OLIVIA
Odious!

JULIO
Pale cheeks, thin lips, and—

OLIVIA
Hold, hold, thou vilifier!

[Throws off her veil; he sinks on one knee.]

There! yes, kneel in contrition for your malicious libel.

JULIO
Say, rather, in adoration. What a charming creature!

OLIVIA
So, now for lies on the other side.

JULIO
A forehead formed by the graces; hair, which cupid would steal for his bow-strings, were he not engaged in shooting through those sparkling hazel circlets, which nature has given you for eyes; lips! that 'twere a sin to call so; they are fresh gathered rose leaves, with the fragrant morning dew still hanging on their rounded surface.

OLIVIA
Is that extemporaneous, or ready cut, for every woman who takes off her veil to you?

JULIO
I believe, 'tis not extemporaneous; for Nature, when she finished you, formed the sentiment in my heart, and there it has been hid, till you, for whom it was formed, called it into words.

OLIVIA
Suppose I should understand, from all this, that you have a mind to be in love with me; would not you be finely caught?

JULIO
Charmingly caught! if you'll let me understand, at the same time, that you have a mind to be in love with me.

OLIVIA
In love with a man! Heavens! I never loved any thing but a squirrel!

JULIO
Make me your squirrel—I'll put on your chain, and gambol and play for ever at your side.

OLIVIA
But suppose you should have a mind to break the chain?

JULIO
Then loosen it; for, if once that humour seizes me, restraint won't cure it. Let me spring and bound at liberty, and when I return to my lovely mistress, tired of all but her, fasten me again to your girdle, and kiss me while you chide.

OLIVIA
Your servant—to encourage you to leave me again?

JULIO
No; to make returning to you, the strongest attraction to my life. Why are you silent?

OLIVIA
I am debating, whether to be pleased or displeased, at what you have said.

JULIO
Well?

OLIVIA
You shall know when I have determined. My friend and yours are approaching this way, and they must not be interrupted.

JULIO
'Twould be barbarous—we'll retire as far off as you please.

OLIVIA
But we retire separately, sir; that lady is a woman of honour, and this moment of the greatest importance to her. You may, however, conduct me to the gate, on condition that you leave me instantly.

JULIO
Leave her instantly—oh, then I know my cue.

[Exit together, R. U. E.

[Enter **CARLOS** L., followed by **VICTORIA**, unveiled.

CARLOS [Looking back on her.]
My wife!

VICTORIA
Oh, Heavens! I will veil myself again. I will hide my face for ever from you, if you will still feast my ears with those soft vows, which, a moment since, you poured forth so eagerly.

CARLOS
My wife!—making love to my own wife!

VICTORIA
Why should one of the dearest moments of my life be to you so displeasing?

CARLOS

So, I am caught in this snare, by way of agreeable surprise, I suppose.

VICTORIA

'Would you could think it so!

CARLOS

No, madam! by Heaven, 'tis a surprise fatal to every hope with which you may have flattered yourself. What! am I to be followed, haunted, watched!

VICTORIA

Not to upbraid you. I followed you because my castle, without you, seemed a dreary desert. Indeed, I will never upbraid you.

CARLOS

Generous assurance! never upbraid me—no, by Heavens! I'll take care you never shall. She has touched my soul, but I dare not yield to the impression. Her softness is worse than death to me! [Aside.]

VICTORIA

'Would I could find words to please you!

CARLOS

You cannot; therefore leave me, or suffer me to go, without attempting to follow me.

VICTORIA

Is it possible you can be so barbarous?

CARLOS

Do not expostulate; your first vowed duty is obedience—that word so grating to your sex.

VICTORIA

To me it was never grating; to obey you has been my joy; even now, I will not dispute your will, though I feel, for the first time, obedience hateful.

[Going, and then turning back.]

Oh, Carlos! My dear Carlos! I go, but my soul remains with you.

[Exit, L.

CARLOS

Oh, horrible! had I not taken this harsh measure, I must have killed myself; for how could I tell her that I have made her a beggar? better she should hate, detest me, than that my tenderness should give her a prospect of felicity, which now she can never taste. Oh, wine-created spirit! where art thou now? Madness, return to me again! for reason presents me nothing but despair.

[Enter **JULIO**, from the top, R. U. E.

JULIO

Carlos, who the devil can they be? my charming little witch was inflexible. I hope yours has been more communicative.

CARLOS

Folly! Nonsense!

JULIO

Folly! Nonsense! What, a pretty woman's smile!—but you married fellows have neither taste nor joy.

CARLOS

Pshaw!

[Crosses, and exit, R.

JULIO

Pshaw! that's a husband! Humph—suppose my fair one should want to debase me into such an animal; she can't have so much villany in her disposition: and yet, if she should? pho! it won't bear thinking about. If I do so mad a thing, it must be as cowards fight, without daring to reflect on the danger.

[Exit, R.

SCENE III.—An Apartment in the House of Don Vasquez, Marcella's Father

Enter **DON CAESAR** and **DON VASQUEZ**, L.

DON CAESAR

Well, Don Vasquez, and a—you—then I say, you have a mind that I should marry your daughter?

DON VASQUEZ

It is sufficient, signor, that you have signified to us your intention—my daughter shall prove her gratitude, in her attention to your felicity.

DON CAESAR

Egad, now it comes to the push! [Aside.] hem, hem!—but just nineteen, you say?

DON VASQUEZ

Exactly, the eleventh of last month.

DON CAESAR

Pity it was not twenty.

DON VASQUEZ

Why, a year can make no difference, I should think.

DON CAESAR

O, yes it does; a year's a great deal; they are so skittish at nineteen.

DON VASQUEZ

Those who are skittish at nineteen, I fear, you won't find much mended at twenty. Marcella is very grave, and a pretty little, plump, fair—

DON CAESAR

Ay, fair again! pity she isn't brown, or olive—I like your olives.

DON VASQUEZ

Brown and olive! you are very whimsical, my old friend!

DON CAESAR

Why, these fair girls are so stared at by the men; and the young fellows, now-a-days, have a damned impudent stare with them—'tis very abashing to a woman—very distressing!

DON VASQUEZ

Yes, so it is; but happily their distress is of that nature, that it generally goes off in a simper. But come, I'll send Marcella to you, and she will—

[Crosses, R.]

DON CAESAR

No, no; stay, my good friend. [Gasping.] You are in a violent hurry!

DON VASQUEZ

Why, truly, signor, at our time of life, when we determine to marry, we have no time to lose.

DON CAESAR

Why, that's very true, and so—oh! St. Antony, now it comes to the point—but there can be no harm in looking at her—a look won't bind us for better for worse. [Aside.] Well, then, if you have a mind, I say, you may let me see her.

[Exit **VASQUEZ**, R.

[**DON CAESAR** puts on his spectacles.]

Ay, here she comes—I hear her—trip, trip, trip! I don't like that step. A woman should always tread steadily, with dignity, it awes the men.

[Enter **VASQUEZ**, leading **MARCELLA**, R.

DON VASQUEZ

There, Marcella, behold your future husband; and remember, that your kindness to him will be the standard of your duty to me.

[Exit, R.

MARCELLA

Oh, Heavens! [Aside.]

DON CAESAR

Somehow, I am afraid to look round.

MARCELLA

Surely he does not know that I am here!

[Coughs gently.]

DON CAESAR

So, she knows how to give an item, I find.

MARCELLA

Pray, signor, have you any commands for me?

DON CAESAR

Hum!—not nonpluss'd at all! [Looks around.] Oh! that eye, I don't like that eye.

MARCELLA

My father commanded me—

DON CAESAR

Yes, I know—I know. [To her.] Why, now I look again, there is a sort of a modest—Oh, that smile; that smile will never do. [Aside.]

MARCELLA

I understand, signor, that you have demanded my hand in marriage.

DON CAESAR

Upon my word, plump to the point! [Aside.] Yes, I did a sort of—I can't say but that I did—

MARCELLA

I am not insensible of the honour you do me, sir, but—but—

DON CAESAR

But!—What, don't you like the thoughts of the match?

MARCELLA

Oh, yes, sir, yes—exceedingly. I dare not say no. [Aside.]

DON CAESAR

Oh, you do—exceedingly! What, I suppose, child, your head is full of jewels, and finery, and equipage? [With ill humour.]

MARCELLA

No, indeed, sir.

DON CAESAR
No, what then? what sort of a life do you expect to lead, when you are my wife? what pleasures d'ye look forward to?

MARCELLA
None.

DON CAESAR
Hey!

MARCELLA
I shall obey my father, sir; I shall marry you; but I shall be most wretched!

[Weeps.]

DON CAESAR
Indeed!

MARCELLA
There is not a fate I would not prefer;—but pardon me!

DON CAESAR
Go on, go on, I never was better pleased.

MARCELLA
Pleased at my reluctance!

DON CAESAR
Never, never better pleased in my life;—so you had really, now, you young baggage, rather have me for a grandfather, than a husband?

MARCELLA
Forgive my frankness, sir—a thousand times!

DON CAESAR
My dear girl, let me kiss your hand.—Egad! you've let me off charmingly. I was frightened out of my wits, lest you should have taken as violent an inclination to the match, as your father has.

MARCELLA
Dear sir, you charm me.

DON CAESAR
But harkye!—you'll certainly incur your father's anger, if I don't take the refusal entirely on myself, which I will do, if you'll only assist me in a little business I have in hand.

MARCELLA

Any thing to show my gratitude.

DON CAESAR
You must know, I can't get my daughter to marry; there's nothing on earth will drive her to it, but the dread of a mother-in-law. Now, if you will let it appear to her, that you and I are driving to the goal of matrimony, I believe it will do—what say you? shall we be lovers in play?

MARCELLA
If you are sure it will be only in play.

DON CAESAR
Oh, my life upon't—but we must be very fond, you know.

MARCELLA
To be sure—exceedingly tender; ha! ha! ha!

DON CAESAR
You must smile upon me, now and then, roguishly; and slide your hand into mine, when you are sure she sees you, and let me pat your cheek, and—

MARCELLA
Oh, no farther, pray; that will be quite sufficient.

DON CAESAR
Gad, I begin to take a fancy to your rogue's face, now I'm in no danger; mayn't we—mayn't we salute sometimes, it will seem infinitely more natural.

MARCELLA
Never! such an attempt would make me fly off at once.

DON CAESAR
Well, you must be lady governess in this business. I'll go home now, and fret madam, about her young mother-in-law—by'e, sweeting!

MARCELLA
By'e, charmer!

DON CAESAR
Oh, bless its pretty eyes!

[Exit, L.

MARCELLA
Bless its pretty spectacles! ha! ha! ha! enter into a league with a cross old father against a daughter! why, how could he suspect me capable of so much treachery? I could not answer it to my conscience. No, no, I'll acquaint Donna Olivia with the plot: and, as in duty bound, we'll turn our arms against Don Cæsar.

[Exit, R.

ACT IV

SCENE I.—Donna Laura's

Enter **DONNA LAURA** and **PEDRO**, R.

LAURA
Well, Pedro, hast thou seen Don Florio?

PEDRO
Yes, Donna.

LAURA
How did he look when he read my letter?

PEDRO
Mortal well; I never see'd him look better—he'd got a new cloak, and a—

LAURA
Pho, blockhead! did he look pleased? did he kiss my name? did he press the billet to his bosom with all the warmth of love?

PEDRO
No, he didn't warm in that way; but he did another, for he put it into the fire.

LAURA
How!

PEDRO
Yes, when I spoke, he started, for, I think, he had forgot that I was by—So, says he, go home and tell Donna Laura, I fly to her presence.

[She waves her hand for him to go.

LAURA
Is it possible? so contemptuously to destroy the letter, in which my whole heart overflowed with tenderness! Oh, how idly I talk! He is here: his very voice pierces my heart! I dare not meet his eye, thus discomposed!

[Exit, R.

Enter **VICTORIA**, L., in men's clothes, preceded by **SANCHA**.

SANCHA

I will inform my mistress that you are here, Don Florio; I thought she had been in this apartment.

[Exit, L.

VICTORIA
Now must I, with a mind torn by anxieties, once more assume the lover of my husband's mistress—of the woman, who has robbed me of his heart, and his children of their fortune. Sure, my task is hard. Oh, love! Oh, married love, assist me! If I can, by any art, obtain from her that fatal deed, I shall save my little ones from ruin, and then—But I hear her step.

[Agitated, pressing her hand on her bosom.]—

There! I have hid my griefs within my heart, and, now for all the impudence of an accomplished cavalier!

[Sings an air, sets her hat in the glass, dances a few steps, &c. then runs to **LAURA**, R., and seizes her hand.]

My lovely Laura!

LAURA
That look speaks Laura loved, as well as lovely.

VICTORIA
To be sure! Petrarch immortalized his Laura by his verses, and mine shall be immortal in my passion.

LAURA
Oh, Florio, how deceitful! I know not what enchantment binds me to thee.

VICTORIA
Me! my dear! is all this to me?

[Playing carelessly with the feather in her hat.

LAURA
Yes, ingrate, thee!

VICTORIA
Positively, Laura, you have these extravagancies so often, I wonder my passion can stand them. To be plain, those violences in your temper may make a pretty relief in the flat of matrimony, child, but they do not suit that state of freedom which is necessary to my happiness. It was by such destructive arts as these you cured Don Carlos of his love.

LAURA
Cured Don Carlos! Oh, Florio! wert thou but as he is?

VICTORIA
Why, you don't pretend he loves you still? [Eagerly.]

LAURA

Yes, most ardently and truly.

VICTORIA

Hah!

LAURA

If thou wouldst persuade me that thy passion is real, borrow his words, his looks: be a hypocrite one dear moment, and speak to me in all the frenzy of that love which warms the heart of Carlos!

VICTORIA

The heart of Carlos!

LAURA

Hah, that seemed a jealous pang—it gives my hopes new life. [Aside.] Yes, Florio, he, indeed, knows what it is to love. For me he forsook a beauteous wife; nay, and with me he would forsake his country.

VICTORIA

Villain! Villain!

LAURA

Nay, let not the thought distress you thus—Carlos I despise—he is the weakest of mankind.

VICTORIA

'Tis false, madam, you cannot despise him. Carlos the weakest of mankind! Heavens! what woman could resist him? Persuasion sits on his tongue, and love, almighty love, triumphant in his eyes!

LAURA

This is strange; you speak of your rival with the admiration of a mistress.

VICTORIA

Laura! it is the fate of jealousy as well as love, to see the charms of its object, increased and heightened. I am jealous—jealous to distraction, of Don Carlos; and cannot taste peace, unless you'll swear never to see him more.

LAURA

I swear, joyfully swear, never to behold or speak to him again. When, dear youth, shall we retire to Portugal?—We are not safe here.

VICTORIA

You know I am not rich.—You must first sell the lands my rival gave you. [Observing her with apprehension.]

LAURA

'Tis done—I have found a purchaser, and to-morrow the transfer will be finished.

VICTORIA [Aside.]

Ah! I have now, then, nothing to trust to but the ingenuity of Gasper. There is reason to fear Don Carlos had no right in that estate, with which you supposed yourself endowed.

LAURA

No right! what could have given you those suspicions?

VICTORIA

A conversation with Juan, his steward, who assures me his master never had an estate in Leon.

LAURA

Never! what, not by marriage?

VICTORIA

Juan says so.

LAURA

My blood runs cold; can I have taken pains to deceive myself?—Could I think so, I should be mad!

VICTORIA

These doubts may soon be annihilated, or confirmed to certainty.—I have seen Don Sancho, the uncle of Victoria; he is now in Madrid.—You have told me that he once professed a passion for you.

LAURA

Oh, to excess; but at that time I had another object.

VICTORIA

Have you conversed with him much?

LAURA

I never saw him nearer than from my balcony, where he used to ogle me through a glass, suspended by a ribbon, like an order of knighthood; he is weak enough to fancy it gives him an air of distinction—Ha! ha! But where can I find him? I must see him.

VICTORIA

Write him a billet, and I will send it to his lodgings.

LAURA

Instantly—Dear Florio, a new prospect opens to me—Don Sancho is rich and generous; and, by playing on his passions, his fortune may be a constant fund to us.—I'll dip my pen in flattery.

[Exit, R.

VICTORIA

Base woman! how can I pity thee, or regret the steps which my duty obliges me to take? For myself, I would not swerve from the nicest line of rectitude, nor wear the shadow of deceit. But, for my children!—Is there a parental heart that will not pardon me?

[Exit, R.

SCENE II.—Don Caesar's

Enter **OLIVIA** and **MINETTE**, R.

OLIVIA
Well, here we are in private—what is this charming intelligence of which thou art so full this morning?

MINETTE
Why, ma'am, as I was in the balcony that overlooks Don Vasquez's garden, Donna Marcella told me, that Don Cæsar had last night been to pay her a visit previous to their marriage, and—

OLIVIA
Their marriage! How can you give me the intelligence with such a look of joy? Their marriage!—what will become of me?

MINETTE
Dear ma'am! if you'll but have patience.—She says that, Don Cæsar and she are perfectly agreed—

OLIVIA
Still with that smirking face?—I can't have patience.

MINETTE
Then, madam, if you won't let me tell the story, please to read it—Here's a letter from Donna Marcella.

OLIVIA
Why did you not give it me at first? [Reads.]

MINETTE
Because I didn't like to be cut out of my story. If orators were obliged to come to the point at once, mercy on us! what tropes and figures we should lose!

OLIVIA
Oh, Minette! I give you leave to smirk again—listen. [Reads.] I am more terrified at the idea of becoming your father's wife, than you are in expectation of a stepmother; and Don Cæsar would be as loath as either of us.—He only means to frighten you into matrimony, and I have, on certain conditions, agreed to assist him; but, whatever you may hear, or see, be assured that nothing is so impossible, as that he should become the husband of Donna Marcella.—Oh, delightful girl! How I love her for this!

MINETTE
Yes, ma'am; and if you'd had patience, I should have told you that she's now here with Don Cæsar, in grave debate how to begin the attack; which must force you to take shelter in the arms of a husband.

OLIVIA
Ah, no matter how they begin it. Let them amuse themselves in raising batteries; my reserved fire shall tumble them about their ears, in the moment my poor father is singing his Io's for victory.—But here

come the lovers—Well, I protest now, sixteen and sixty is a very comely sight.—'Tis contrast gives effect to every thing.—Lud! how my father ogles! I had no idea he was such a sort of man. I am really afraid he isn't quite so good as he should be!

[Enter **DON CAESAR**, leading **MARCELLA**, L.

DON CAESAR
H—um! Madam looks very placid; we shall discompose her, or I am mistaken. [Apart.] So, Olivia, here's Donna Marcella come to visit you—though, as matters are, that respect is due from you.

OLIVIA
I am sensible of the condescension. My dear ma'am, how very good this is!

[Taking her hand.]

DON CAESAR
Yes, you'll think yourself wonderfully obliged, when you know all! [Aside.] Pray, Donna Marcella, what do you think of these apartments?—The furniture and decorations are my daughter's taste; would you wish them to remain, or will you give orders to have them changed?

MARCELLA
Changed, undoubtedly; I can have nobody's taste govern my apartments but my own.

DON CAESAR
Ah that touches!—See how she looks!—[Apart.] They shall receive your orders.—You understand, I suppose, from this, that every thing is fixed on between Donna Marcella and me?

OLIVIA
Yes, sir; I understand it perfectly; and it gives me infinite pleasure.

DON CAESAR
Eh! pleasure?

OLIVIA
Entirely, sir—

DON CAESAR
Tol-de-rol! Ah, that wont do—that wont do! You can't hide it.—You are frightened out of your wits at the thoughts of a mother-in-law; especially a young, gay, handsome one.

OLIVIA
Pardon me, sir; the thought of a mother-in-law was indeed disagreeable; but her being young and gay qualifies it.—I hope, ma'am, you'll give us balls, and the most spirited parties.

[Crosses, C.]

You can't think how stupid we have been. My dear father hates those things; but I hope now—

DON CAESAR

Hey! hey! hey! what's the meaning of all this? Why, hussy, don't you know you'll have no apartment but the garret?

OLIVIA

That will benefit my complexion, sir, by mending my health. 'Tis charming to sleep in an elevated situation.

DON CAESAR

Here! here's an obstinate perverse slut!

OLIVIA

Bless me, sir, are you angry that I look forward to your marriage without murmuring?

DON CAESAR

Yes, I am—yes, I am; you ought to murmur; and you ought to—to—to—

OLIVIA

Dear me! I find love, taken up late in life, has a bad effect on the temper.—I wish, my dear papa, you had felt the influence of Donna Marcella's charms somewhat sooner.

DON CAESAR

You do! you do! why this must be all put on.—This can't be real.

OLIVIA

Indeed, indeed it is; and I protest, your engagement with this lady has given me more pleasure than I have tasted ever since you began to tease me about a husband. You seem determined to have a marriage in the family; and I hope, now, I shall live in quiet, with my dear, sweet, young mother-in-law.

DON CAESAR

Oh! oh! [Walking about.] Was there ever—[Crosses, C.] She doesn't care for a mother-in-law!—Can't frighten her!

OLIVIA

Sure, my fate is very peculiar; that being pleased with your choice, and submitting, with humble duty, to your will, should be the cause of offence.

DON CAESAR

Hussy! I don't want you to be pleased with my choice—I don't want you to submit with humble duty to my will.—Where I do want you to submit, you rebel: you are a—you are—But I'll mortify that wayward spirit, yet.

[Exit **DON CAESAR** and **MARCELLA**, R.

MINETTE

Well, really, my master is in a piteous passion; he seems more angry at your liking his marriage, than at your refusing to be married yourself.—Wouldn't it have been better, madam, to have affected discontent?

OLIVIA

To what purpose, but to lay myself open to fresh solicitations, in order to get rid of the evil I pretended to dread? Bless us! Nothing can be more easy than for my father to be gratified, if he were but lucky in the choice of a lover.

MINETTE

As much as to say, madam, that there is—

OLIVIA

Why, yes, as much as to say—I see you are resolved to have my secret, Minette, and so—

[Enter **SERVANT**, L.

SERVANT

There is a gentleman at the door, madam, called Don Julio de Melessina. He waits on you from Don Vincentio.

OLIVIA

Who? Don Julio! it cannot be—art thou sure of his name?

SERVANT

The servant repeated it twice. He is in a fine carriage, and seems to be a nobleman.

OLIVIA

Conduct him hither.

[Exit **SERVANT**, L.]

I am astonished! I cannot see him! I would not have him know the incognita to be Olivia, for worlds!—There is but one way. [Aside.] Minette, ask no questions; but do as I order you.—Receive Don Julio in my name; call yourself the heiress of Don Cæsar; and on no account suffer him to believe that you are any thing else.

[Exit, R.

MINETTE

So, then, this is some new lover she is determined to disgust; and fancies, that making me pass for her will complete it. Perhaps her ladyship may be mistaken though.—[Looking through the wing.]—Upon my word a sweet man! Oh, lud! my heart beats at the very idea of his making love to me, even though he takes me for another! Stay! I think he shan't find me here. Standing in the middle of a room gives one's appearance no effect. I'll enter upon him with an easy swim, or an engaging trip, or a—something that shall strike—the first glance is every thing.

[Exit, R.

Enter **DON JULIO**, L., preceded by a **SERVANT**, who retires, R.

JULIO

Not here! The ridiculous dispute between Garcia and Vincentio gives me irresistible curiosity; though, if she is the character Garcia describes, I expect to be cuffed for my impertinence.—Here she comes!—A pretty, smiling girl, 'faith, for a vixen!

[Enter **MINETTE**, R., very affectedly.

MINETTE

Sir, your most obedient humble servant.—You are Don Julio de Melessina. I am extremely glad to see you, sir.

JULIO [Aside.]

A very courteous reception!—You honour me infinitely, madam. I must apologize for waiting on you without a better introduction. Don Vincentio promised to attend me; but a concert called him to another part of the town, at the moment I prepared to come hither.

MINETTE

A concert—Yes, sir, he is very fond of music.

JULIO

He is, madam:—You, I suppose, have a passion for that charming science?

MINETTE

Oh, yes, I love it mightily.

JULIO [Aside.]

This is lucky! I think I have heard, Donna Olivia, that your taste that way is peculiar; you are fond of a—'faith, I can hardly speak it, [Aside.]—of a—Jew's-harp.

[Smothering a laugh.]

MINETTE

A Jew's-harp! Mercy! What, do you think a person of my birth and figure, can have such fancies as that?—No, sir, I love fiddles, French horns, tabors, and all the cheerful, noisy instruments in the world.

JULIO [Aside.]

Vincentio must have been mad; and I as mad as he, to mention it. Then you are fond of concerts, madam?

MINETTE

Dote on them! I wish he'd offer me a ticket. [Aside.]

JULIO [Aside.]

Vincentio is clearly wrong.—Now to prove how far the other was right, in supposing her a vixen.

MINETTE

There is a grand public concert, sir, to be to-morrow. Pray, do you go?

JULIO

I believe I shall have that pleasure, madam.

MINETTE

My father, Don Cæsar, won't let me purchase a ticket: I think it's very hard.

JULIO

Pardon me—I think it's perfectly right.

MINETTE

Right! what, to refuse me a trifling expense, that would procure me a great pleasure?

JULIO

Yes, doubtless—the ladies are too fond of pleasure: I think Don Caesar is exemplary.

MINETTE

Lord, sir! you'd think it very hard, if you were me, to be locked up all your life; and know nothing of the world but what you could catch through the bars of your balcony.

JULIO

Perhaps I might; but, as a man, I am convinced 'tis right. Daughters and wives should be equally excluded those destructive haunts of dissipation. Let them keep to their embroidery, nor ever presume to show their faces but at their own firesides.—This will bring out the Xantippe, surely! [Aside.]

MINETTE

Well, sir, I don't know—to be sure, home, as you say, is the fittest place for women. For my part, I could live for ever at home. I am determined he shall have his way; who knows what may happen? [Aside.]

JULIO [Aside.]

By all the powers of caprice, Garcia is as wrong as the other!

MINETTE

I delight in nothing so much as in sitting by my father, and hearing his tales of old times; and I fancy, when I have a husband, I shall be more happy to sit and listen to his stories of present times.

JULIO

Perhaps your husband, fair lady, might not be inclined so to amuse you. Men have a thousand delights that call them abroad; and probably your chief amusements would be counting the hours of his absence, and giving a tear to each as it passed.

MINETTE

Well, he should never see them, however. I would always smile when he entered; and if he found my eyes red, I'd say, I had been weeping over the history of the unfortunate damsel, whose true love hung himself at sea, and appeared to her after wards in a wet jacket.—Sure, this will do! [Aside.]

JULIO

I am every moment more astonished. Pray, madam, permit me a question. Are you, really—yet I cannot doubt it—are you, really, Donna Olivia, the daughter of Don Cæsar, to whom Don Garcia and Don Vincentio had lately the honour of paying their addresses?

MINETTE
Am I Donna Olivia! ha! ha! ha! what a question! Pray, sir, is this my father's house?—Are you Don Julio?

JULIO
I beg your pardon; but, to confess, I had heard you described as a lady who had not quite so much sweetness, and—

MINETTE
Oh! what, you had heard that I was a termagant, I suppose.—'Tis all slander, sir: there is not in Madrid, though I say it, a sweeter temper than my own; and though I have refused a good many lovers, yet, if one was to offer himself that I could like—

JULIO
You would take pity, and reward his passion.

MINETTE
I would.

JULIO
Lovely Donna Olivia, how charming is this frankness!—'Tis a little odd, though! [Aside.]

MINETTE
Why, I believe I should take pity: for it always seemed to me to be very hard-hearted, to be cruel to a lover that one likes, because, in that case, one should—a—you know, sir, the sooner the affair is over, the better for both parties.

JULIO
What the deuce does she mean?—Is this Garcia's sour fruit?

DON CAESAR [Without, R.]
Olivia! Olivia!

MINETTE
Bless me, I hear my father! Now, sir, I have a particular fancy that you should not tell him, in this first visit, your design.

JULIO
Madam, my design!

MINETTE
Yes, that you will not speak out, till we have had a little further conversation, which I'll take care to give you an opportunity for very soon. He'll be here in a moment: now, pray, Don Julio, go. If he should meet you, and ask who you are, you can say, that you are—you may say, that you came on a visit to my maid, you know.

[Exit, R.

JULIO
I thank you, madam, [Aloud.] for my dismission. [Aside.] I never was in such a peril in my life. I believe she has a license in her pocket, a priest in her closet, and the ceremony by heart.

[Exit.

ACT V

SCENE I.—Don Carlo's

DON CARLOS discovered writing.

CARLOS [Tearing paper, and rising.]
It is in vain!—Language cannot furnish me with terms, to soften to Victoria the horrid transaction. Could she see the compunctions of my soul, her gentle heart would pity me. But what then?—She's ruined! my children are undone! Oh! The artifices of one base woman, and my villany to another most amiable one, have made me unfit to live. I am a wretch, who ought to be blotted from society.

[Enter **PEDRO**, hastily, L.

PEDRO
Sir—sir!

CARLOS
Well!

PEDRO
Sir, I have just met Don Florio; he asked if my mistress was at home; so I guesses he is going to our house, and so I run to let you know—for I loves to keep my promises, though I am deadly afraid of some mischief.

CARLOS
You have done well.—Go home, and wait for me at the door, and admit me without noise.

[Exit **PEDRO**, L.]

At least, then, I shall have the pleasure of revenge; I'll punish that harlot, by sacrificing her paramour in her arms; and then—Oh!

[Exit, L.

SCENE II.—Donna Laura's

Enter **LAURA**, L., with precipitation, followed by **VICTORIA**.

LAURA
'Tis his carriage!—How successful was my letter! This, my Florio, is a most important moment.

VICTORIA
It is, indeed; and I will leave you to make every advantage of it.

[Crosses, R.]

If I am present, I must witness condescensions from you, that I shall not be able to bear, though I know them to be but affected.—Now, Gasper, [Aside.] play thy part well, and save Victoria!

[Exit, R.

[Enter **GASPER**, L. dressed as an old Beau; two **SERVANTS** follow him, and take off a rich cloak.

GASPER
Take my cloak; and, d'ye hear, Ricardo, go home and bring the eider-down cushions for the coach, and tell the fellow not to hurry me post through the streets of Madrid.

[Exeunt **SERVANTS**, L.]

I have been jolted from side to side, like a pippin in a mill stream. Drive a man of my rank, as he would a city vintner and his fat wife, going to a bull fight! Ha, there she is!

[Looking through a glass, suspended by a red ribbon.]

—there she is! Charming Donna Laura! let me thus at the shrine of your beauty—

[Makes an effort to kneel, and falls on his face; **LAURA** assists him to rise.]

Fie, fie, those new shoes!—they have made me skate all day, like a Dutchman on a canal; and now—Well, you see how profound my adoration is, madam. Common lovers kneel; I was prostrate.

LAURA
You do me infinite honour.—Disgustful wretch!—You are thinner than you were, Don Sancho: I protest, now I observe you, you are much altered!

GASPER
Ay, madam—fretting. Your absence threw me into a fever, and that destroyed my bloom:—You see, I look almost a middle-aged man, now.

LAURA
No, really; far from it, I assure you.—The fop is as wrinkled as a baboon! [Aside.]

GASPER

Then jealousy—that gave me a jaundice.—My niece's husband, I hear, Don Carlos, has been my happy rival. Oh, my blade will hardly keep in its scabbard, when I think of him.

LAURA

Think no more of him—he has been long banished my thoughts, be assured. I wonder you gave your niece to him, with such a fortune.

GASPER

Gave! she gave herself; and, as to fortune, she had not a pistole from me.

LAURA

'Twas, indeed, unnecessary, with so fine an estate as she had in Leon.

GASPER

My niece an estate in Leon! Not enough to give shelter to a field-mouse; and if he has told you so, he is a braggart.

LAURA

Told me so—I have the writings; he has made over the lands to me.

GASPER

Made over the lands to you!—Oh, a deceiver! I begin to suspect a plot. Pray, let me see this extraordinary deed.

[She runs to a Cabinet, D. F.]

A plot, I'll be sworn!

LAURA

Here is the deed which made that estate mine for ever. No, sir, I will intrust it in no hand but my own. Yet look over me, and read the description of the lands.

GASPER [Reading through his glass.]

H—m—m—. In the vicinage of Rosalvo, bounded on the west by the river—h—m—m, on the east by the forest—Oh, an artful dog! I need read no further; I see how the thing is.

LAURA

How, sir!—but hold—Stay a moment—I am breathless with fear.

GASPER

Nay, madam, don't be afraid! 'Tis my estate—that's all; the very castle where I was born; and which I never did, nor ever will, bestow on any Don in the two Castiles. Dissembling rogue! Bribe you with a fictitious title to my estate—ha! ha! ha!

LAURA [Aside.]

Curses follow him! The villain I employed must have been his creature; his reluctance all art; and, whilst I believed myself undoing him, was duped myself!

GASPER

Could you suppose I'd give Carlos such an estate for running away with my niece? No, no; the vineyards, and the cornfields, and the woods of Rosalvo, are not for him.—I've somebody else in my eye—in my eye, observe me—to give those to:—Can't you guess who it is?

LAURA

No, indeed!—He gives me a glimmering that saves me from despair! [Aside.]

GASPER

I won't tell you, unless you'll bribe me—I won't indeed.

[Kisses her cheek.]

There, now I'll tell you—they are all for you. Yes, this estate, to which you have taken such a fancy, shall be yours.—I'll give you the deeds, if you'll promise to love me, you little, cruel thing!

LAURA

Can you be serious?

GASPER

I'll sign and seal to-morrow.

LAURA

Noble Don Sancho! Thus, then, I annihilate the proof of his perfidy, and my weakness.—Thus I tear to atoms his detested name; and as I tread on these, so would I on his heart.

[Enter **VICTORIA**, R.

VICTORIA

My children then are saved! [In transport.]

LAURA [Apart.]

Oh, Florio, 'tis as thou saidst—Carlos was a villain, and deceived me.—Why this strange air? Ah, I see the cause—you think me ruined, and will abandon me. Yes, I see it in thy averted face; thou dar'st not meet my eyes. If I misjudge thee, speak!

VICTORIA

Laura, I cannot speak.—You little guess the emotions of heart.—Heaven knows, I pity you!

LAURA

Pity! Oh, villain! and has thy love already snatched the form of pity? Base, deceitful—

CARLOS [Without.]

Stand off; loose your weak hold; I'm come for vengeance!

[Enter **CARLOS**, L.

Where is this youth? Where is the blooming rival, for whom I have been betrayed? Hold me not, base woman! In vain the stripling flies me; for, by Heaven, my sword shall in his bosom write its master's wrongs!

[**VICTORIA** first goes towards the Flat, then returns, takes off her hat, and drops on one knee.

VICTORIA
Strike, strike it here! Plunge it deep into that bosom, already wounded by a thousand stabs, keener and more painful than your sword can give. Here lives all the gnawing anguish of love betrayed; here live the pangs of disappointed hopes, hopes sanctified by holiest vows, which have been written in the book of Heaven.—Hah! he sinks.—

[She flies to him.]

—Oh! my Carlos! beloved! my husband! forgive my too severe reproaches; thou art dear, yet dear as ever, to Victoria's heart!

CARLOS [Recovering.]
Oh, you know not what you do—you know not what you are. Oh, Victoria, thou art a beggar!

VICTORIA
No, we are rich, we are happy! See there, the fragments of that fatal deed, which, had I not recovered, we had been indeed undone; yet still not wretched, could my Carlos think so!

CARLOS
The fragments of the deed! the deed which that base woman—

VICTORIA
Speak not so harshly.—To you, madam, I fear, I seem reprehensible; yet, when you consider my duties as a wife and mother, you will forgive me. Be not afraid of poverty—a woman has deceived, but she will not desert you!

LAURA
Is this real? Can I be awake?

VICTORIA
Oh, may'st thou indeed awake to virtue!—You have talents that might grace the highest of our sex; be no longer unjust to such precious gifts, by burying them in dishonour.—Virtue is our first, most awful duty; bow, Laura! bow before her throne, and mourn in ceaseless tears, that ever you forgot her heavenly precepts!

LAURA
So, by a smooth speech about virtue, you think to cover the injuries I sustain. Vile, insinuating monster!—but thou knowest me not.—Revenge is sweeter to my heart than love; and if there is a law in Spain to gratify that passion, your virtue shall have another field for exercise.

[Exit, R.

CARLOS [Turning towards **VICTORIA**.]

My hated rival and my charming wife! How many sweet mysteries have you to unfold?—Oh, Victoria! My soul thanks thee, but I dare not yet say I love thee, till ten thousand acts of watchful tenderness, have proved how deep the sentiment's engraved.

VICTORIA

Can it be true that I have been unhappy?—But the mysteries, my Carlos, are already explained to you—Gasper's resemblance to my uncle—

GASPER

Yes, sir, I was always apt at resemblances—In our plays at home, I am always Queen Cleopatra—You know she was but a gipsey queen, and I hits her off to a nicety.

CARLOS

Come, my Victoria—Oh, there is a painful pleasure in my bosom—To gaze on thee, to listen to and to love thee, seems like the bliss of angels' cheering whispers to repentant sinners.

[Exeunt **CARLOS** and **VICTORIA**, L.

GASPER

Lord help 'em! how easily the women are taken in!

[Exit, L.

SCENE III.—The Prado

Enter **MINETTE**, L.

MINETTE

Ah, here comes the man at last, after I have been sauntering in sight of his lodgings these two hours. Now, if my scheme takes, what a happy person I shall be! and sure, as I was Donna Olivia to-day, to please my lady, I may be Donna Olivia tonight, to please myself. I'll address him as the maid of a lady who has taken a fancy to him, then convey him to our house—then retire, and then come in again, and, with a vast deal of confusion, confess I sent my maid for him. If he should dislike my forwardness, the censure will fall on my lady; if he should be pleased with my person, the advantage will be mine. But perhaps he's come here on some wicked frolic or other.—I'll watch him at a distance before I speak.

[Exit, L. U. E.

[Enter **DON JULIO**, R.

JULIO

Not here, 'faith; though she gave me last night but a faint refusal, and I had a right, by all the rules of gallantry, to construe that into an assent.—Then she's a jilt. Hang her, I feel I am uneasy—The first woman that ever gave me pain—I am ashamed to perceive that this spot has attractions for me, only because it was here I conversed with her. 'Twas here the little syren, conscious of her charms, unveiled her fascinating face—'Twas here—Ha!

[Enter **DON GARCIA** and **DON VINCENTIO**, R. U. E.

GARCIA
Ha! Don Julio!

JULIO
Pshaw! gentlemen, pray be quick.

GARCIA
'Twas here that Julio, leaving champaigne untasted, and songs of gallantry unsung, came to talk to the whistling branches.

VINCENTIO
'Twas here that Julio, flying from the young and gay, was found in doleful meditation—[Altering his tone.]—on a wench, for a hundred ducats!

GARCIA
Who is she?

JULIO
Not Donna Olivia, gentlemen; not Donna Olivia.

GARCIA
We have been seeking you, to ask the event of your visit to her.

JULIO
The event has proved that you have been most grossly duped.

VINCENTIO
I know that—Ha! ha! ha!

JULIO
And you likewise, I know that—Ha! ha! ha!—The fair lady, so far from being a vixen, is the very essence of gentleness. To me, so much sweetness in a wife, would be downright mawkish.

VINCENTIO
Well, but she's fond of a Jew's-harp.

JULIO
Detests it; she would be as fond of a Jew.

GARCIA
Pho, pho! this is a game at cross purposes;—let us all go to Don Cæsar's together, and compare opinions on the spot.

JULIO

I'll go most willingly—But it will be only to cover you both with confusion, for being the two men in Spain most easily imposed on.

[All going, R.

[Enter **MINETTE**, L.

MINETTE

Gentlemen, my lady has sent me for one of you, pray which of you is it?

JULIO [Returning.]

Me, without doubt, child.

VINCENTIO

I don't know that.

GARCIA

Look at me, my dear; don't you think I am the man?

MINETTE

Let me see—a good air, and well made—you are the man for a dancer. [To **GARCIA**.]—Well dressed, and nicely put out of hands—you are the man for a bandbox.

[Crosses to **VINCENTIO**.]

—Handsome and bold—you are the man for my lady.

[Crosses to **JULIO**.]

JULIO

My dear little Iris, here's all the gold in my pocket. Gentlemen, I wish you a good night—I am your very obedient, humble—

[Stalking by them, with his arm round **MINETTE**.

GARCIA

Pho! pr'ythee, don't be a fool. Are we not going to Donna Olivia?

JULIO

Donna Olivia must wait, my dear boy; we can decide about her to-morrow. Come along, my little dove of Venus!

[Exit, L.

GARCIA

What a rash fellow it is! ten to one but this is some common business, and he'll be robbed and murdered—they take him for a stranger.

VINCENTIO

Let's follow, and see where she leads him.

GARCIA

That's hardly fair: however, as I think there's danger, we will follow.

[Exit, L.

SCENE IV.—Don Caesar's

Enter **MINETTE** and **DON JULIO**, L.

MINETTE

There, sir, please to sit down, till my lady is ready to wait on you—she won't be long—I'm sure she's out, and I may do great things before she returns. [Aside.—

[Exit, R.

JULIO

Through fifty back lanes, a long garden, and a narrow staircase, into a superb apartment—all that's in the regular way; as the Spanish women manage it, one intrigue is too much like another. If it was not now and then for the little lively fillip of a jealous husband or brother, which obliges one to leap from a window, or crawl, like a cat, along the gutters, there would be no bearing the ennui. Ah! ah! but this promises novelty; [Looking through the Wing.] a young girl and an old man—wife or daughter? They are coming this way. My lovely incognita, by all that's propitious! Why did not some kind spirit whisper to me my happiness? but hold—she can't mean to treat the old gentleman with a sight of me.

[Goes behind the sofa.

Enter **DON CAESAR** and **OLIVIA**, L.

DON CAESAR

No, no, madam, no going out—There, madam, this is your apartment, your house, your garden, your assembly, till you go to your convent. Why, how impudent you are to look thus unconcerned!—Can hardly forbear laughing in my face!—Very well—very well!

[Exit, double locking the door, L.

OLIVIA

Ha! ha! ha! I'll be even with you, my dear father, if you treble lock it. I'll stay here two days, without once asking for my liberty, and you'll come the third, with tears in your eyes, to take me out.—He has forgot the door leading to the garden—but I vow I'll stay. [Sitting down.] I can make the time pass pleasantly enough.

JULIO

I hope so.

[Looking over the back of the sofa.

OLIVIA
Heaven and earth!

JULIO
My dear creature, why are you so alarmed? am I here before you expected me?

[Coming round, R.

OLIVIA
Expected you!

JULIO
Oh, this pretty surprise! Come, let us sit down; I think your father was very obliging to lock us in together.

OLIVIA
Sir! sir! my father!

[Calling at the door.

DON CAESAR [Without.]
Ay, 'tis all in vain—I won't come near you. There you are, and there you may stay. I shan't return, make as much noise as you will.

JULIO
Why, are you not ashamed that your father has so much more consideration for your guest than you have?

OLIVIA
My guest! how is it possible he can have discovered me? [Aside.]

JULIO
Pho! This is carrying the thing further than you need—if there was a third person here, it might be prudent.

OLIVIA
Why, this assurance, Don Julio, is really—

JULIO
The thing in the world you are most ready to pardon.

OLIVIA
Upon my word, I don't know how to treat you.

JULIO
Consult your heart!

OLIVIA
I shall consult my honour.

JULIO
Honour is a pretty thing to play with, but when spoken with that very grave face, after having sent your maid to bring me here, is really more than I expected. I shall be in an ill humour presently—I won't stay if you treat me thus.

[Crosses, L.]

OLIVIA
Well, this is superior to every thing! I have heard that men will slander women privately to each other; 'tis their common amusement; but to do it to one's face!—and you really pretend that I sent for you?

JULIO
Ha! ha! ha! Well, if it obliges you, I will pretend that you did not send for me; that your maid did not conduct me hither; nay, that I have not now the supreme happiness—

[Catching her in his arms.

[Enter **MINETTE**; she screams, and runs out, R.

JULIO
Donna Olivia de Zuniga! how the devil came she here?

OLIVIA [Aside.]
That's lucky! Olivia, my dear friend, why do you run away? Keep the character I charge you. [Apart to **MINETTE**.] Be still Olivia.

MINETTE
Oh! dear madam! I was—I was so frightened when I saw that gentleman.

OLIVIA
Oh, my dear; it's the merriest pretty kind of gentleman in the world; he pretends that I sent my maid for him into the streets, ha! ha!

JULIO
That's right; always tell a thing yourself, which you would not have believed.

MINETTE
It is the readiest excuse for being found in a lady's apartment, however. Now will I swear I know nothing of the matter. [Aside.]

OLIVIA

Now, I think it a horrid poor excuse; he has certainly not had occasion to invent reasons for such impertinencies often. Tell me that he has made love to you to-day. [Apart.]

MINETTE
I fancy that he has had occasion to excuse impertinencies often;—his impertinence to me to-day—

JULIO
To you, madam?

MINETTE
Making love to me, my dear, all the morning—could hardly get him away, he was so desirous to speak to my father. Nay, sir, I don't care for your impatience.

JULIO [Aside.]
Now would I give a thousand pistoles if she were a man!

OLIVIA
Nay, then, this accidental meeting is fortunate—pray, Don Julio, don't let my presence prevent your saying what you think proper to my friend—shall I leave you together? [Crosses, L.]

JULIO [Apart.]
To contradict a lady on such an assertion would be too gross; but, upon my honour, Donna Olivia is the last woman upon earth who could inspire me with a tender idea. Find an excuse to send her away, my angel, I entreat you. I have a thousand things to say, and the moments are too precious to be given to her.

OLIVIA
I think so too, but one can't be rude, you know. Come, my dear, sit down, [Seating herself, C.] have you brought your work?

JULIO
The devil! what can she mean?

[Pushing himself between **MINETTE** and the sofa.]

Donna Olivia, I am sorry to inform you that my physician has just been sent for to your father, Don Caesar.—The poor gentleman was seized with a vertigo.

OLIVIA
Vertigoes! Oh, he has them frequently, you know. [To **MINETTE**.]

MINETTE
Yes, and they always keep me from his sight.

JULIO
Did ever one woman prevent another from leaving her at such a moment before? I really, madam, cannot comprehend—

DON CAESAR [Without.]
It is impossible—impossible, gentleman! Don Julio cannot be here.

JULIO
Hah! who's that?

Enter **DON CAESAR**, **DON GARCIA**, and **DON VINCENTIO**, L. D.

GARCIA
There! did we not tell you so? we saw him enter the garden.

DON CAESAR
What can be the meaning of all this? A man in my daughter's
apartment!

[Attempting to draw.]

GARCIA
Hold, sir! Don Julio is one of the first rank in Spain, and will unquestionably be able to satisfy your
honour, without troubling your sword. We have done mischief, Vincentio! [Apart.]

JULIO [To **OLIVIA**.]
They have been cursedly impertinent! but I'll bring you off, never fear, by pretending a passion for your
busy friend, there.

DON CAESAR
Satisfy me then in a moment; speak, one of you.

[Crosses to **JULIO**.]

JULIO
I came here, sir, by the merest accident.—The garden door was open, curiosity led me to this
apartment. You came in a moment after, and very civilly locked me in with your daughter.

DON CAESAR
Locked you in! why, then, did you not, like a man of honour, cry out?

JULIO
The lady cried out, sir, and you told her you would not return; but when Donna Olivia de Zuniga entered,
for whom I have conceived a most violent passion—

DON CAESAR
A passion for her! Oh, let me hear no more on't.—A passion for her! You may as well entertain a passion
for the untameable hyena.

GARCIA
There, Vincentio, what think you now? Xantippe or not?

VINCENTIO
I am afraid I must give up that—but pray support me as to this point, Don Cæsar; is not the lady fond of a Jew's-harp?

DON CAESAR
Fond! she's fond of nothing, but playing the vixen; there is not such a fury upon earth.

JULIO
These are odd liberties, with a person who does not belong to him.

DON CAESAR
I'll play the hypocrite for her no more; the world shall know her true character, they shall know—but ask her maid there.

JULIO
Her maid!

MINETTE
Why, yes, sir; to say truth, I am but Donna Olivia's maid, after all.

OLIVIA [Apart.]
Dear Minette! speak for me, or I am now ruined.

MINETTE
I will, ma'am.—I must confess, sir, [Going up to **JULIO**.] there never was so bitter a tempered creature as my lady is. I have borne her humours for two years; I have seen her by night and by day.

[**OLIVIA** pulls her sleeve, impatiently.]

I will, I will! [To **OLIVIA**.] and this I am sure, that if you marry her, you'll rue the day every hour the first month, and hang yourself the next. There, madam, I have done it roundly now.

[Exit, R.]

OLIVIA
I am undone—I am caught in my own snare! [Aside.]

DON CAESAR
After this true character of my daughter, I suppose, signor, we shall hear no more of your passion; so let us go down, and leave madam to begin her penance.

JULIO
My ideas are totally confused.—You Donna Olivia de Zuniga, and the person I thought you, her maid! something too flattering darts across my mind.

DON CAESAR
If you have taken a fancy to her maid, I have nothing farther to say; but as to that violent creature—

JULIO

Oh, do not profane her. Where is that spirit which you tell me of? Is it that which speaks in modest, conscious blushes on her cheeks? Is it that which bends her lovely eyes to earth?

DON CAESAR

Ay, she's only bending them to earth, considering how to afflict me with some new obstinacy—she'll break out like a tigress in a moment.

JULIO

It cannot be—are you, charming woman! such a creature?

OLIVIA

Yes, to all mankind—but one. [Looking down.]

JULIO

But one! Oh, might that excepted one, be me!

OLIVIA

Would you not fear to trust your fate with her, you have cause to think so hateful?

JULIO

No, I'd bless the hour that bound my fate to hers. Permit me, sir, to pay my vows to this fair vixen.

DON CAESAR

What, are you such a bold man as that? Pho! but if you are, 'twill be only lost time—she'll contrive, some way or other, to return your vows upon your hands.

OLIVIA

If they have your authority, sir, I will return them—only with my own.

DON CAESAR

What's that! what did she say? my head is giddy with surprise.

JULIO

And mine with rapture.

[Catching her hand.

DON CAESAR

Don't make a fool of me, Olivia.—Wilt marry him?

OLIVIA

When you command me, sir.

DON CAESAR

My dear Don Julio, thou art my guardian angel—shall I have a son-in-law at last? Garcia, Vincentio, could you have thought it?

GARCIA

No, sir; if we had, we should have saved that lady much trouble; 'tis pretty clear now, why she was a vixen.

VINCENTIO

Yes, yes, 'tis clear enough, and I beg your pardon, madam, for the share of trouble I gave you—but, pray, have the goodness to tell me sincerely, what do you think of a crash?

[Crosses to **OLIVIA**.

OLIVIA

I love music, Don Vincentio, I admire your skill, and whenever you'll give me a concert, I shall be obliged.

[Crosses to **DON CAESAR**.

VINCENTIO

You could not have pleased me so well, if you had married me.

[Enter **DON CARLOS** and **VICTORIA**, R.

OLIVIA

Hah! here comes Victoria and her Carlos. My friend, you are happy—'tis in your eyes; I need not ask the event.

DON CAESAR

What, is this Don Carlos, whom Victoria gave us for a cousin? Sir, you come in a happy hour.

CARLOS

I do indeed, for I am most happy.

JULIO

My dear Carlos, what has new made thee thus, since morning?

CARLOS

A wife! Marry, Julio, marry!

JULIO

What! this advice from you?

CARLOS

Yes; and when you have married an angel, when that angel has done for you such things, as makes your gratitude almost equal to your love, you may then guess something of what I feel, in calling this angel mine.

OLIVIA

Now, I trust, Don Julio, after all this, that if I should do you the honour of my hand, you'll treat me cruelly, be a very bad man, that I, like my exemplary cousin—

VICTORIA

Hold, Olivia! it is not necessary that a husband should be faulty, to make a wife's character exemplary.—Should he be tenderly watchful of your happiness, your gratitude will give a thousand graces to your conduct; whilst the purity of your manners, and the nice honour of your life, will gain you the approbation of those, whose praise is fame.

OLIVIA

Pretty and matronly! thank you, my dear. We have each struck a bold stroke to-day;—yours has been to reclaim a husband, mine to get one: but the most important is yet to be obtained—the approbation of our judges.

That meed withheld, our labours have been vain;
Pointless my jests, and doubly keen your pain;
Might we their plaudits, and their praise provoke,
Our bold should then be term'd, a happy stroke.

DISPOSITION OF THE CHARACTERS AT THE FALL OF THE CURTAIN.

DON CAESAR.	DONNA OLIVIA.
DON VASQUEZ.	DON JULIO.
DON GARCIA.	DON CARLOS.
DON VINCENTIO.	DONNA VICTORIA.

R.]   [L.

Hannah Cowley – A Short Biography

Hannah Cowley was born Hannah Parkhouse on March 14th, 1743, the daughter of Hannah (née Richards) and Philip Parkhouse, a bookseller in Tiverton, Devon.

As one might expect details of much of her life are scant and that of her early life almost non-existent.

However, we do know that she married Thomas Cowley in either 1768 or 1772 and that the marriage produced 3 or perhaps 4 children.

The couple moved to London after their marriage and Thomas worked as an official in the Stamp Office and as a part-time journalist.

Her career in the literary world seemed to happen rather late. It was whilst the couple were attending a play, thought to be sometime in late 1775, that Cowley was struck by a sudden necessity to write. "So delighted with this?" she boasted to him. "Why I could write as well myself!"

And she set to work. By the next day she showed him the first act of her comedy; The Runaway. She set about finishing the rest of the play and then sent it to the famed actor-manager, David Garrick. It was produced at his final season at the Drury Lane theatre on February 15th, 1776.

The Runaway enjoyed 17 performances in its first season at Drury Lane and was revived many times thereafter.

Its initial success, and the encouragement of the newly retired Garrick, ensured that Cowley would write more. She wrote her next two plays, the farce, Who's the Dupe? and the tragedy, Albina, before the year was out.

Who's the Dupe? and Albina encountered several difficulties getting into production. The new manager of Drury Lane, Richard Brinsley Sheridan, postponed The Runaway for most of the 1777 season. Upset, Cowley thought of an alternate means to get her play produced. She sent Albina to Drury Lane's rival theatre in London, Covent Garden. Alas it was not accepted. Albina now bounced back and forth between the two theatres for the next two years. Meanwhile, Sheridan agreed to produce Who's the Dupe? but the premiere would only take place in the spring, an unprofitable time for a new play to open.

The play brought controversy. Her rival Hannah More had written Percy and it opened in 1777. Cowley thought several parts of it were similar to her own, as yet, un-produced play. It raised her suspicions. When Hannah More next had The Fatal Falsehood open in 1779 Cowley was convinced that More had plagarised from her own Albina.

Indeed when The Fatal Falsehood opened on May 6th, 1779, it was followed by charges in the press that More stole her ideas from Cowley. On August 10th, More wrote to the St. James Chronicle to protest that she "never saw, heard, or read, a single line of Mrs. Cowley's Tragedy." Cowley herself was hurt but acted with good grace. She wrote in a later printed preface to Albina that hers and More's plays do indeed have "wonderful resemblances." And she allowed that theatre managers, who in those days also acted as script editors, may have inadvertently given More her ideas: "Amidst the crowd of Plots, and Stage Contrivances, in which a Manager is involv'd, recollection is too frequently mistaken for the suggestions of imagination"

Albina finally opened on July 31st, 1779, at the Haymarket to neither financial nor critical success.

With the Hannah More controversy behind her, Cowley wrote her most popular comedy, The Belle's Stratagem. It was staged at Covent Garden in 1780. In its first season it performed for 28 nights and was regularly revived helping to ensure a solid revenue stream for Cowley and her family.

Her next play, The World as It Goes; or, a Party at Montpelier (the title was later changed to Second Thoughts Are Best) was unsuccessful, but she continued to write and there followed another seven plays; Which is the Man?; A Bold Stroke for a Husband; More Ways Than One; A School for Greybeards, or, The Mourning Bride; The Fate of Sparta, or, The Rival Kings; A Day in Turkey, or, The Russian Slaves and The Town Before You.

Sadly, none could recreate her initial triumph.

In 1783, Thomas Cowley accepted a job with the British East India Company and left for India leaving his wife in London to continue her career and to raise their children. Thomas never returned to England and died in India in 1797.

As well as plays Cowley also wrote poetry. In 1786, she wrote "The Scottish Village, or Pitcairne Green".

In 1787, under pseudonym "Anna Matilda," she and the poet Robert Merry (under his own pseudonym of "Della Crusca") began a poetic correspondence through the pages of The World journal. The poems were sentimental and flirtatious. Initially they did not even know the others' identity; but they later met and became part the Della Cruscans poetry movement. This volume of poetry was published under her pseudonym in 1788 as The Poetry of Anna Matilda.

Cowley's last play, The Town Before You, was produced in 1795.

In 1801 Cowley published perhaps her greatest poetical work. A six-book epic "The Siege of Acre: An Epic Poem".

That same year Cowley retired to Tiverton in Devon, where she spent her remaining years out of the public spotlight whilst she quietly revised her plays.

In her day, Cowley's works were popular and thought provoking. One critic noted she was "one of the foremost playwrights of the late eighteenth century" whose "skill in writing fluid, sparkling dialogue and creating sprightly, memorable comic characters compares favourably with her better-known contemporaries, Goldsmith and Sheridan."

Hannah Cowley died of liver failure on March 11th, 1809.

Hannah Cowley – A Concise Bibliography

Plays
The Runaway (1775, Staged 1776)
Who's the Dupe? (1776, Staged 1779)
Albina (1776, Staged 1779)
The Belle's Stratagem (1780)
The World as It Goes; or, a Party at Montpelier
Which is the Man?
A Bold Stroke for a Husband (1783)
More Ways Than One
A School for Greybeards, or, The Mourning Bride
The Fate of Sparta, or, The Rival Kings
A Day in Turkey, or, The Russian Slaves
The Town Before You (1795)

Poetry
The Scottish Village, or Pitcairne Green (1786)

The Poetry of Anna Matilda (A pseudonym) includes A Tale for Jealousy and The Funeral (1788)
The Siege of Acre: an Epic Poem (1801)

Scenarios of Some of Her Plays

The Runaway (1776)

George Hargrave, who is home from college, is overjoyed to learn that Emily, the mysterious runaway whom his godfather, Mr. Drummond, has taken in, is the same young lady he fell in love with at a recent masquerade. Meanwhile, George's spirited cousin, Bella, helps George's sister, Harriet, and George's friend Sir Charles fall in love. George's designs are threatened when he learns that his father wants George to marry Lady Dinah, a pretentious older lady who is also very rich. When Emily's father arrives to take Emily back to London, George gives chase and snatches Emily back. Mr. Drummond saves the day by offering the young lovers some of his land so that they can have a fortune of their own.

Who's the Dupe? (1779)

Granger, a captain, arrives in town to see his lover, Elizabeth. Her uneducated father, Abraham Doiley, has promised her hand to the most educated man he can find, an unappealing but intelligent scholar named Gradus. Elizabeth's friend Charlotte, who fancies Gradus for herself, persuades Gradus to act more fashionable and less bookish so that he can win Elizabeth's heart. Doiley is not impressed by the new Gradus; meanwhile, Granger presents himself to Doiley as a scholar so that he can win Elizabeth's hand. Granger and Gradus square off against each other to see who is the more educated, and Granger wins by using phony Greek that nonetheless impresses Doiley. Gradus is consoled by winning Charlotte.

Albina (1779)

The powerful Duke of Westmorland learns that the gallant young soldier Edward is in love with his daughter, Albina, who is a young widow to Count Raimond. Despite her love for Edward, Albina's virtue impedes her from agreeing to marry him. Westmorland and Edward persuade her to remarry because Edward is soon destined to go off to war; she agrees. Editha, who is jealous of Albina, seeks help from Lord Gondibert, Raimond's brother, who secretly loves Albina. On the eve of the wedding, Gondibert tells Edward that Albina has been unfaithful, and to prove it he disguises himself and allows Edward to spy on him sneaking into Albina's chamber at night. Edward then calls off the wedding, and the furious Westmorland challenges him to a duel to protect Albina's honour. Before the duel begins, Gondibert's elderly servant, Egbert, exposes his master's lie, and the king banishes Gondibert. Before he leaves, Gondibert vows to kill Albina and then commit suicide. He sneaks into Albina's chamber and stabs a woman he thinks is Albina, and then he stabs himself. But the woman turns out to be a disguised Editha, who had also stolen into the room. Edward is relieved when the real Albina rushes into the room, and the dying Gondibert asks for and receives her pardon.

The Belle's Stratagem (1780)

Having returned from his trip to Europe, the handsome Doricourt meets his betrothed, Letitia. He finds her acceptable but by no means as elegant as European women. Determined that she will not marry without love, Letitia enlists the help of her father, Mr. Hardy, and Mrs. Racket, a widow, to turn Doricourt off the wedding by pretending that she, Letitia, is an unmannerly hoyden. Meanwhile, Doricourt's friend Sir George is being overprotective of his new wife, Lady Frances, who rebels and agrees to accompany Mrs. Racket for a day in the town and a masquerade ball that night. While out at an auction, Lady Frances meets the rake, Courtall, who brags to his friend Saville that he will seduce her.

Meanwhile, Letitia's brazen acting succeeds in dissuading Doricourt from wanting to marry her. All characters converge at that night's masquerade. The disguised Letitia shows off her charms, bewitches Doricourt and then leaves before he can find out who she is. Courtall, disguised the same way as Sir George, lures the lady he thinks is Lady Frances back to his house. However, Saville has replaced the real Lady Frances with a prostitute who is disguised as Lady Frances is. Shamed, Courtall leaves town. The next day, Doricourt, who has been told that Mr. Hardy is on his deathbed, visits him and reluctantly agrees to marry Letitia after all. Then the disguised Letitia enters and reveals her true identity to the overjoyed Doricourt, who also learns that Hardy was not ill after all.

A Bold Stroke for a Husband (1783)
Set in Madrid, the play tells of Don Carlo, who has fled his wife, Victoria, for the courtesan Laura. Laura breaks off with Don Carlo, but she holds on to the documents that entitle her to his land, a gift he foolishly gave her. We learn that Laura is in love with Florio, who is really Victoria disguised as a young man. Meanwhile, Victoria's friend Olivia is resisting efforts by her father, Don Caesar, to marry her off to a series of suitors. In desperation, Don Caesar pretends that he will marry and young girl and then send Olivia off to a convent unless she marries right away. Victoria persuades Olivia's servant to disguise himself as her rich uncle, the original owner of the land that Laura now holds. He convinces Laura that the titles are worthless, so in a rage she rips them up. Victoria reveals herself to Don Carlos, who repents and pledges himself to her again. Meanwhile, Olivia gets married to Julio, the man she wanted all along.